Independent London/ Store Guide.

Dear Independent shopper,

Congratulations! You are obviously an independent thinker and have made an inspired choice, thank you for buying the first edition of our guide to the best independent* shops in London; shops set up and run by individuals living in your community. Our book is a small contribution but we hope that by highlighting what's best in the local community we can perhaps rekindle some sorely lacking community spirit. We hope you enjoy our book and it helps you rediscover your London. For our next even better guide we invite you to send us your favourite independent shops of any kind, in your area. We want to showcase these shop keepers for doing a good job and reward their efforts! Be independent!

submit@independentlondon.com

*In today's globalised world the word 'independent' has perhaps more resonance than ever before. In a time where its easier to buy a fruit from Africa than from locally produced growers, where people from those countries starve, while agricultural production is destroyed in the UK in addition to the environmental damage caused by the movement of all these goods.

Britain, a nation of shop keepers…
but where are they all? Working at Tescos?

With 2000 local shops closing a year in Britain (since the end of world war two the number of small shops has plunged from 500,000 to 30,000) enough is enough.

We know you know where Boots, Snappy Snaps and the other (insert name here) clone high street shops are but where's the Flea-Pit or F-Art or La Bouche? Well they're all here in this little gem. Your Independent Store Guide is our way to inform you of all that's individual, artesan, creative, eclectic and just great, as well as of course independent – independent of mind, spirit, and soul.

'Clone town' is a threat to diversity, the environment the very social fabric of Britain, its time to redress the balance so we want to show you the best in Independent shopping around London. We can't promise free parking, trolleys and long queues and 2 for 1 offers but with our detailed descriptions and photographs we can help you find the best individual shopping in London. Be Independent.

Moritz Steiger & Effie Fotaki, Independent London.

Contents

Shop
Categories

Identify the colour of the kind of store that takes your fancy to reference the map and inividual pages at a glance.

**Green//
Health/**
*Therapy,
Spas,
Beauty.*

**Grey//
Art/**
Galleries.

Yellow//
Home/
Furniture,
Kitchen,
Design,
Bathroom.

Pink//
Entertain-
ment /
DVD's,
Music,
Books, Bikes,
Leisure time.

Blue//
Fashion/
Style,
Clothes,
Shoes,
Jewellery.

Orange//
Flowers/
Plants.

Purple//
Food/
Cafes,
Bars,
Deli's,
Restaurants.

interesting venue

cafe

pub

market

wi-fi

restaurants

museum

underground

Geffrye museum

Shoreditch Town Hall

Old Street

Shoreditch

Broadgate

Spitalfields

Map 1

8

100m

Buses: 26 from waterloo,
55 from Tottenham ct.Rd
Nearest tubes: Shoreditch,
Old street, Liverpool street

What's There/

Internet/wireless (wi-fi):
coffee@ (internet),
LCB Surf Store (wi-fi, café)
Cafes: Macondo, The Hookah
Lounge. **Pubs/bars:** The Redchurch.
Restaurants: The Flea Pit. **Markets:**
Spitalfields, Fri,Sat, Sun. Brick
LaneBrick-a-Brack, Sunday all day.
Flower Market, Columbia Rd, Sunday
till 2pm.

Culture/

Festivals: Spitalfields festival, Aug.
Spitalfields winter festival,
Dec 12-21. Brick Lane Festival, 2nd
Sunday Sept, yearly. Brick Lane
Curry Festival, 5 September. **Places
of Interest:** Galleries around Viner
St, Cambridge Heath. Denis Sever's
house at 18 Folgate St. Shoreditch
Town Hall. **Museums/ Galleries:**
Rich Mix (cinema and exhibitions)
35-47 Bethnal Green Rd. Geffrye
Museum, Kingsland Rd. **Parks:**
Hoxton Square. Haggerston Park.

Hoxton, Shoreditch, Spitalfields, Broadway Market, Columbia Road.

'The Ditch' and Hoxton, now so synonymous with urban cool, is a great haven for independent businesses of all kinds from art galleries to bike shops. Take a stroll through our shop listing starting with the market in Spitalfields and finishing in the Cat & Mutton in Broadway market. Be independent.

Map 1
No.1

A-non Clothing
26 Cheshire Street
E2 6EH

T: 020 7729 2144

www.a-non.co.uk

Open/
10am-6pm,
Mon-Sat;
10am-5pm, Sun

A-non Clothing

It's hard to imagine that just over 50 years ago wearing a T-shirt would have been seen as shocking. From its humble beginning as underwear, the T-shirt has become an enduring fashion staple, from the cool of James Dean to hippie tie-dye. Today it's just as important a part of any fashionista's wardrobe as your local chav's. A-non's crams in plenty of racks of the ubiquitous top. Much of it should appeal to those children of the Eighties with plenty referencing old TV shows and film stars (Mr T as Clubber Lang from Rocky 2 anyone?), all to be worn with a mild smirk of irony. Feel like you need a bit of punk in your wardrobe? Grab a Ramones or The Clash t-shirt, although you'll have to distress it properly yourself. And for those who want a witty slogan that gets less funny with every read there's plenty here to amuse, for a while.

Artwords Bookshop

A small white cuboid, Artwords Bookshop is the quintessential design and visual art bookshop in stock and in appearance. Tucked into Rivington Street, one of the main arteries of Shoreditch, there are plenty of words and pictures to delight, distract and amuse the local community of creatives, fashion victims and poseurs. From the latest one-off style mags to gorgeously glossy hard backs the cool white interior keeps up it's refined appearance by not cramming too much in, but has choice selections. You should be able to find anything from books on typography to David LaChapelle's latest extravagance. If you can't, ask, staff aren't too cool for school and happy to help track down a book, or if needs be, order it.

Entertain-ment//

Map 1
No.2

Artwords
Bookshop
65A Rivington
Street
EC2A 3QQ

T:020 7729 2000

Open/
11am-7pm,
Mon-Sat

Map 1
No.3

74 Broadway
Market, London,
E8 4J

T: 020 7923 9450
www.blacktruffle.
com

Open/
11am-6pm,
Tues-Fri;
10am-6pm, Sat;
noon-6pm, Sun

Black Truffle

Snuffle out this cute boutique on Broadway market for rare delicacies of contemporary bags and chichi shoes from lesser-known designers. It's one of the few stockists of Lumi bags and best sellers Matt & Nat's hold-alls. Apparently, they fly off the shelves because of their hip style rather than their ethical credentials of being completely vegan. Owner Melissa Needham is also an accessories designer and her stock reflects her fun and stylish taste, without Blahnik prices. Other rare gems that should appeal to ce-roc revivalists and those that desire a touch of movie starlet glamour are heels from Repetto, a traditional French company that make dance shoes - Brigitte Bardot was known to have worn a pair.

La Bouche

A little piece of France in north London, this deli and café is a honey pot for the gourmands, local artists and creative loafers who have moved into the area in the last few years. The tiny premises is full with all manner of goodies from jars of fish soup and marons imported from the mother country, to freshly baked bread and a fantastic selection of cheeses. The French proprietor Stef actually started out with a cheese stall on the farmers market that takes place on Saturdays. He still has it, as there just isn't enough space on the shelves for all the stock (space has been found though for a photo of Thierry Henry behind the counter). It's also a great spot for a cup of contemplative freshly ground coffee – careful, its rocket fuel - a sandwich or pastry, especially on a sunny day sitting at one of the outside tables.

Food//

Map 1
No.4

La Bouche
49 Broadway
Market
E8 4PH
T: 020 7812 9912
www.labouche.
co.uk

Open/
8.30am-7pm
Mon- Fri;
8.30am-5pm, Sat;
10am-4pm, Sun

Bob & Blossom
140 Columbia Rd
E2

T: 020 7739 4737

Open/
9am-3pm, Sun

Bob & Blossom

If you manage to fight your way through the foliage of Columbia Road on a market day, you'll find some blooming marvellous gear for children at Bob and Blossom. There are smart togs here for babies and toddlers, we're not talking Little Lord Fauntleroy style, but from continental and British labels like Mitty James, they're a cut above t-shirts reading 'mother sucker'. There is plenty of fun stuff as well, traditional toys, and a fantastic range of Babar Papa products – the strange pink blob cartoon character that parents of little ones today might remember from their own childhood. They're all presented in a refined, uncluttered interior with an air of panache.

Brick Lane Bikes

Bring them your multi-speeds, your horizontal drop-outs and your bone-shakers, Brick Lane Bikes will repair them all. But what they really do is build fixed-wheel machines – that's a bike with a fixed gear and possibly no breaks. Commuters without a death wish can have breaks fitted and any specification can be catered for. The advantage of fixed-wheel bikes is weight reduction – so saddle up and maybe it can help your own weight reduction regime or just speed up your commute or track time. A full bike from Terry Dolan starts at around £550. Italian track and tour specialists Guerciotti frames and components are also stocked for the serious rider. Owner Jan Milewski and his charming staff are happy to give a free diagnosis of any sickly bikes. Ride on, man.

Entertain-ment//

Map 1 No.6

Brick Lane Bikes
118 Bethnal Green
Road
E2
T:020 7033 9053
www.
bricklanebikes.
co.uk

Open/
9am-8.30pm,
Mon-Fri;
11am-8.30pm, Sat;
11am- 7pm, Sun

Map 1 No.7

The Cat and Mutton
76 Broadway Market
E8 4QJ

www. catandmutton. co.uk

Open/
6am-11pm Mon;
noon-11pm,
Tue-Sat;
noon-10.30pm,
Sun

The Cat and Mutton

There have be some additions to Hackney's burgeoning gastro pub scene in the last few years, but this, the area's original bringer of good food and drink to the area's middle classes, has been holding its own well. An unfussy interior with simple sturdy furniture is well-used by the locals hungry for the British and European food, wine and ale, and the place is often packed on Friday and Saturday nights. The dog and child-friendly policy ensures that it attracts young families, so weekend daytimes can seem a little bit like a boozy crèche. There's a scattering of art on the wall in main part of the pub, resolutely managed by Kevin Cooper. Upstairs lies The Cat Studio, a large and light space often used for exhibitions and events.

Close-up

Damien Sanville, the French owner of this film-savant's paradise, used to be a champion of local film-making talent. He used to sell local film makers' films on DVD, but stopped, "because they were shit," says Damien with his gallic deadpan. "Nearly all of them could have been entitled 'Me and My Camera'." He's serious about film, but there's also a seriously impressive selection of world cinema, classics, experimental film and documentaries for rental and sale. There are some concessions to Hollywood releases to keep the cash register ticking over, but the main aim of Damien, himself a writer and film-maker, is to create an archive of film and one day open a local independent cinema. It opened in August 2005 and judging by the stacked shelves of DVDs covering the bare-brick walls he's well on his way to his aim of 12,000 titles. Naturally all are organised by director and country for film buffs' delectation.

Entertain-
ment//

Map 1
No.8

Close-up
139 Brick Lane
E1 6SB

T: 020 7739 3634

www.close-
upvideos.com

Open/
Noon-10pm
Mon-Sun

Map 1
No.9

Comfort Station
22 Cheshire Street
E2 6EH

T: 020 7033 9099

www.
comfortstation.
co.uk

Open/
11am-6pm,
Fri-Sun;
by appointment,
Mon-Thur

Comfort Station

A delightful boutique that appears to draw more inspiration from Alice Through the Looking Glass than Voyage. Suspended above the black and white stripped floor hangs a chandelier and against the walls old leather suitcases hang open to display the shop's collection of jewellery. While there's a hint of old world charm and elegance about everything, all the pretty little earrings, tops and handbags are newly designed, and reflecting the shop's décor, deserving a closer inspection. The silk bracelets are chic and with a twist. Get closer to the stuffed magpie in flight (there's an owl, too) to discover the cut-glass dangly earrings it's clutching in its talons have little notes attached, reading things like, 'I want cake' and 'There's no place like home'. It's a shop that indulges your sense of fantasy rather than suspends it.

Ella Doran

Ella Doran has made quite a name for herself with her ranges of digital prints on soft furnishings and homeware – she has a range of products made for Tate St Ives. Her new store, along the increasingly creative hum that is Cheshire Street is also her studio with a small space at the front displaying her latest collections. From the creative workshop downstairs emerge bold, bright florals to complement the range of stripes and stacks on coasters, place mats, cushions and bags. A bespoke blind service is also available to add lightness to darkness. Having established herself she is now championing new young designer such as Emma Jeffs and her decorative window film.

Home//

Map 1
No.10

Ella Doran
46 Cheshire Street
E2 6EH

T: 020 7613 0782

www.elladoran.
co.uk

Open/
10am-6pm,
Thur,Fri;
noon-5pm, Sat;
11am-6pm, Sun

19

F-art Galleries
24 Cheshire Street
E2 6EH
T:020 7729 5411
www.f-art.uk.com
Open/
Noon- 5pm, Sat;
10am- 5pm, Sun

F-art Galleries

John Lennon may have been the first to be quoted referring to something as "art with a capital F", but this refined shop gets the joke in early so you don't have to. F-art is a bit of a curate's egg, all the better for the self-awareness of its own pretentions. Come here if you fancy something a bit different, basically. We're not talking a microlite or an alpenhorn (sadly), but prints, paintings by co-owner Stephen Davids and other independent artists or idiosyncratic pieces of furniture or original 1950s film posters. Recent additions to the shop floor have included a 1968 Castelli porcelain bowl and a G-Plan Danish armchair – both had a nicely balanced quirky retro flavour and are incredibly stylish. Like it says on the giant chalk board behind the counter covered with random scribbles, "It's good to be bonkers."

Far Global

This Columbia Road store is a showcase for non-European, old and antique furniture that hails from further east than Bethnal Green. Most of the pieces come from Rajasthan, South India and Africa and are sourced by owner Marc Snell, who has combined his background in furniture design with a love of travelling to south and east Asia. He owned a concession in Selfridges prior to opening this store, but has since been able to add more pieces as well as curios, tribal art and masks to the treasure trove. As interested in the aesthetic value of the pieces as the mystique and story behind the designs, Marc will happily fill in any potential customer with the history behind the pieces they are interested in.

Home//

Map 1
No.12

Far Global
124 Columbia
Road
E2

T: 07931151663

www.farglobal.
co.uk

Open/
9am-4pm, Sun;
by appointment,
Mon-Sat

Food//

Map 1
No.13

The Grocery
54- 56 Kingsland
Road
E2 8DP

www.
thegroceryshop.
co.uk

Open/
8am-7pm,
every day

The Grocery

Where supermarkets fear to tread -and there can't be many places left- The Grocery has stepped in to fill the gap and stack the shelves with everything you could possibly want. Championing unprocessed, seasonal and organic products -but not beholden to an earth mother philosophy - you will find anything from some fine British cheeses to cans of beans and light bulbs. Owner Joff Goodman worked in numerous jobs, from software to antiques before starting this venture with business partner Simon Hill, a former chef who brought in his love of good food to the shop.

The Flea-Pit

Comfortably careworn, there's usually a laid-back vibe at this popular local café and arts space, where the organic light bites and beers from the menu can be sampled on what looks to be auntie's best 1970s crockery. More than just a café, tricked out with free broadband for the slews of late twenty and thirty-somethings that regularly slough on the shabby chic sofas, there's an exhibition space behind the main room. Exhibitions change monthly and are curated by local art pros Tom Wilmott and Bob London who are always on the lookout for new talent. If that wasn't enough there are many other events that serve to get the locals attention away from their organic coffee - free film screenings of documentaries, poetry readings, live music and even knitting circles – most of them costing nowt extra.

Food//

Map 1 No.14

The Flea-Pit
49 Columbia Road
E2 7RG

T: 020 7033 9986

www.thefleapit.
com

Open/
3.30-11pm,
Tues, Wed;
11.30am-11pm,
Thur-Sat;
9.30am-2pm, Sun

Murdock
340 Old Street
EC1V 9DS

T: 020 7729 2288

www.
murdocklondon.
com

Open/
11am-7pm,
Mon-Wed;
11am-8pm,
Thur, Fri;
10am-6pm, Sat

Murdock

Owner Brendan Murdock decided it was about time someone smartened up the scruffs of Shoreditch. Frustrated by the lack of a welcoming men's grooming salon with traditional values of service and excellence, he opened his self-named man space, having cut his teeth in the area with local restaurant CRU. The attention given to the stylish interior with red leather barbers chairs extends to the full-range of grooming services and the products used; Murdock has a more idiosyncratic approach than many more self-consciously trendy barbers with a range encompassing the quintessentially English D.R Harris as well as extreme sports-tested Californian brand, Brave Soldier. Retail is also a feature of the store with the addition of vintage books and copies of Playboy to the grooming products. Also functioning as a gallery space for East End artists, the stuffed animals of taxidermist Polly Morgan and designer, Laura Lees have recently added another facet to this great space.

Glorias

Sneaker peepers and trainer twitchers will get their kicks here. The place for high-end trainers from the main players of Adidas, Nike and Reebok as well as smaller brands. Owners Matt Paton and Offer Zeloof source the shoes from all over the world, as well as attracting clientele from across the globe, and often secure exclusive limited edition pairs. Recent additions to the all-star line up have been JB from the US and Feit from Australia, both relatively unknown to British buyers. And what else does an urban trainer junky need as well as a pair of rare Adidas adicolors? Cool toys of course. Cartoonist James Jarvis' World of Pain figurines take pride of place in the glass cabinet at the back of the split level store, and there's more youth culture related ephemera and toys from Kubrick and Pete Fowler's Monsterism collection.

Fashion//

Map 1 No.16

Glorias
6 Dray Walk
The Old Brewery
91 Brick Lane
E1 6QL

T: 020 7770 662

www.superdeluxe. net

Open/
10am-7pm, every day

Map 1
No.17

Hurwundeki
98 Commercial
Street
E1 6LZ

T:020 73929194

www.hurwundeki.
com

Open/
11am-7pm;
Mon-Fri;
10am-7pm,
Sat, Sun

Hurwundeki

Hurwundeki's Korean owner opened this vintage and second hand clothes store in 2004 originally with a hairdressers at the back and space for photography exhibitions. That's been given the chop now with the focus on vintage designer clothes. Upstairs is the bulk of the second-hand men's and women's clothing with a selection of new clothes as well. A great place to find a silk cravat or pair of leather gloves if you're a man about town. The basement is like an elegant dressing up box, housing the shop's Edwardian and Victorian clothes and other vintage designer items from Chanel shoes to velvet capes. There are plans afoot to augment the stock with Hurwundeki's own designer label.

Junky Styling

Having recently graced the sofa of Richard and Judy, Kerry Seager and Annika Sanders are now big time. They started out making clothes for themselves to go clubbing in during the early 1990s. After getting so much attention they decided to turn their hobby into a business. And very successful it's been, too. Not that providing outfits for Gwen Stefani, Sadie Frost or Russell Brand with their unique style of ethical millinery isn't impressive enough, but their focus is less on celebrity and more on creating affordable, unique items with an emphasis on sustainability. All pieces are 'recycled' from old clothes and material and turned into something new and vibrant. Men's and women's clothes get the treatment with old stock sources from closed factories in the UK and US. A bespoke service called 'wardrobe surgery' is offered, where you can bring in an old top to be restyled or remodelled in to something, individual new and wonderful.

Fashion//

Map 1
No.18

Junky Styling
12 Dray Walk,
The Old Brewery,
91 Brick Lane
E1 6RF

T: 020 7247 1883

www.junkystyling.
co.uk

Open:
10.30am-6.30pm,
Mon-Fri;
11am-6.30pm,
Sat, Sun

Labour and Wait
16 Cheshire Street
E2 6EH

T:020 7729 6253

www.
labourandwait.
co.uk

Open/
11am-5pm, Fri;
1-5pm, Sat;
10am-5pm, Sun

Labour and Wait

Walk in here and you'll be forgiven for thinking that the last half of the twentieth century never happened. With a standpoint that everyday classics will not date, but improve with age, Labour and Wait is a trove of practical household goods that have stood the test of time. Looking past the brown paper packages tied up with string in the window, it's clear that some of the favourite things here are garden tools and a range of enamel kitchenware. You can even dress like a 1950s artisan with their range of striped shirts and chunky woollen socks – all the stock here is sourced from across Europe by existing manufacturers. Alessi then is a dirty word, although some French soap flakes (£6.50) would soon clean your mouth out. Their only concession to the twenty first century is an online shop.

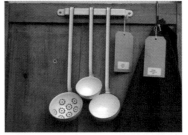

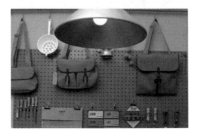

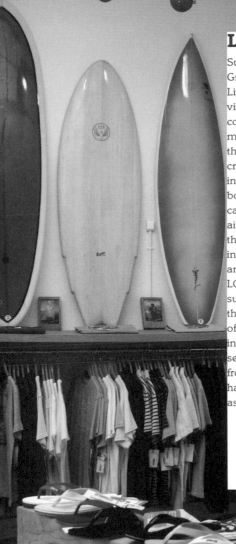

LCB Surf

Surf is most definitely up on Bethnal Green Road. Cousins Mark and Pete Lindsell have brought the laid back vibe of the surfing scene and their considerable passion and talent for making custom made boards to the East End. After learning their craft in Portugal, the pair specialise in making short and retro shaped boards. But however you want it they can do it, be it with stencil art or an airbrushed ninja decoration riding the halfpipe. They're branching out to include snowboards and skateboards and their partners have expanded LCB with a new line in clothing. If surfing the internet is more your thing than gnarly gear, have a cup of organic java in the shops café and internet area. All that lovely oak you see in the shop and café was made from one tree by Mark and Pete's hands in their previous incarnation as tree surgeons.

Fashion//

Map 1
No.20

LCB Surf
121 Bethnal Green
Road
E2 7DG

T: 020 7739 3839

www.lcbsurff.com

Open/
8am-8pm,
every day

Lik Neon
106 Sclater Street
E1 6HR

T:07876 323 265

www.likneon.com

Open/
Noon-7pm, Mon;
11am-7pm,
Tue-Sat;
11am-6.30pm, Sun

Lik Neon

Despite its appearance as suffering from a shop version of attention deficit disorder, Lik Neon is trying to focus as much as it can on clothing and jewellery by new designers, such as owner Janice Taylor's hand-shaped Perspex bangles and necklaces, produced by her own jewellery label, FFP. As well as the experimental design, if you're a fan of old travel Mastermind games, Thundercats action figures and other bits of jumble from the last few decades of the twentieth century, you'll love this wilfully quirky shop where everything has a hand-written price sticker. It's a bit like a trendy Shoreditch teenager's bedroom crossed with a car boot sale. Among the 'vintage' items that augment the fashion and jewellery, lies a retro and experimental record collection, the latter of which contains some rare and limited edition vinyl.

Macondo

The enchanted fictional town where the Buendia family lived in Gabriel Garcia Marquez's 100 Years of Solitude can now be found in Hoxton Square. It's a site for flights of fancy and cocktails rather than malingering ghosts and doomed love affairs, but Pablo Casas and his business partners have certainly injected some Latin American flavour to the area. Half Mexican, Pablo has ensured that the house speciality, its range of margaritas are mixed with the finest Mexican tequila and that the happy hour is always just that. To complement the cocktails (the sours are also worth a try) there's a menu that brings the best of South and Central America to locals' plate, from Bolivian tortillas (that's not local slang) to Argentinean empanadas. Add to the mix an ever-changing exhibition of art, photography or experimental weirdness from young local artists on the walls and Mexican pottery and you can fiesta in a very Shoreditch manner.

Food//

Map 1
No.22

Macondo
8 & 9 Hoxton
Square
N1 6NU

T: 020 7729 1119

www.macondo.
co.uk

Open/
9.30am-11pm,
Mon-Thur, Sun;
9.30am-midnight,
Fri, Sat

Miame
172 Brick Lane
E1 6RU

T: 020 7650 8873

www.miame.
co.uk

Open/
11am-7pm,
Mon-Wed;
11am-8pm
Thur- Sun

Miame

A shop with a split personality and two different types of customer to match. The ground floor space is home to an eclectic collection of tunes on vinyl and CD that should keep any Shoreditch DJ in rapture. The range encompasses plenty of mainstream genres from house to hip hop and everything in between. If the ground floor is home to flocks of nodding vinyl junkies and bedroom b-boys, upstairs turns its attention to fashion. The focus, if you can see through the coterie of Brick Lane trendies, is on women's clothes and an emphasis on one off pieces. Many are from young, local fashion designers. There is also a made to measure service for those wanting that extra dash of exclusivity. Miame is named after the man himself, the shop's owner and principle character. He trained as a designer, but his family have been in the rag trade for generations, so it really is in his jeans.

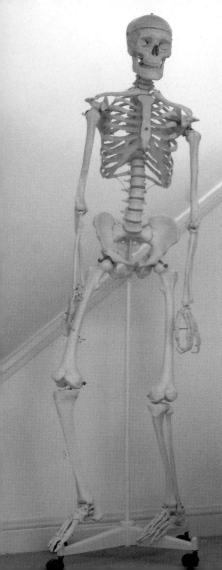

Osteopathy

Osteopathy has been easing the pain of locals since 2004 with the help of Rick Harter's healing hands. He originally trained in shiatsu before undertaking the five years of training needed to become a certified osteopath. As such he has an holistic approach to manipulation, and while not explicitly part of the treatments, adds in his previous knowledge of the Japanese therapeutic massage and its focus on energy systems during the hour-long sessions. Offering a drop-in service, Rick is joined by a colleague who specialises in cranial osteopathy, which is recommended for babies and children. As if he isn't qualified enough, Rick is embarking on an MA in Pain Management, so as well as being a master of manipulation he will also be a master of pain, which if the treatment wasn't so beneficial, would make him sound like someone you'd want to avoid.

Health//

**Map 1
No.24**

Oteopathy
14A Broadway
Market
E8
T: 020 7249 2866

Open/
9am-5pm, Mon;
9am-9pm,
Tue,Thur;
9am-1pm,
Wed, Fri, Sat

Map 1
No.25

Pimps & Pinups
14 Lamb St
E1 1EA

T: 020 7426 2121

www.
pimpandpinups.
com

Open/
10am-7am,
Mon-Fri;
11am-6pm
Sat, Sun

Pimps & Pinups

Cousins James and Simon Chamson came over from Adelaide in south Australia in 2002 and fours years later have found themselves running this increasingly successful boutique hairdresser in Spitalfields Old Market. Simon has the cutting credential and James brought his marketing nous to the operation. The result is salon with 1950s Hollywood glamour. The mirrors ringed by light bulbs and retro Japanese chairs have started to attract the area's glitterati - Pete Doherty has walked past and gawped through the window on a number of occasions. Perhaps unsurprisingly he's yet to walk in for a colour and cut by the salon's multi-national staff. The focus is on fun, but also raw hairdressing.

Queens

Depending on who you are, you might describe this emporium in Spitalfields indoor market as either an enchanted fairytale come to life, or a camp cavern of kitsch, it's certainly unlike any other store in London. Step inside and you're accosted by thousands or dangly fairies, teddy bears, dolls and twee and scented gifts. It's crammed in from floor to ceiling, and some might find it a bit too much, but if you're looking for Christmas tree decorations any time of the year, this is definitely the place to come. Queens has been here for eight years and in that time seen the reconstruction of Spitalfields market. Thankfully, it's housed in the protected area, so they'll always be a place for those.

Home//

**Map 1
No.26**

Queens
Shop 111B
Old Spitalfields
Market
E1 6BG

T: 020 7426 0017

Open/
11.30-6pm
Tue-Fri;
11am-5pm Sat;
10am-6pm Sun

Story
3 Dray Walk
91 Brick Lane
E1 6QL

T: 020 7247 3137

Open:
8.30am- 4.30pm,
Mon-Fri;
8.30am-6pm,
Sat, Sun

Story Delicatessen

Owner Lee Hollingworth was twenty years ahead of his time. In 1983 he opened an organic food shop, but expensive, weird-looking veg didn't catch on back then. Now however, things are booming. Lee and his partner Ann Shore opened this deli in January 2004, having already run a successful lifestyle interiors shop of the same name. Everything is certified 100 per cent organic, from the breakfasts to the chocolate puddings and mineral water, and made on the premises by Lee, Ann and their colleagues – Lee is the self-confessed salad guru. Pizza is their other big thing, having found it nearly impossible themselves, to find anywhere in the area that made a really good pizza. While Lee has ideas to become the Prêt a Manger of organic deli, this is no cynical marketing ploy, Lee and Ann live the life themselves and invite others to do the same.

Shangri-La

Get inked by Lesley Chan, one of the sweetest tattooists you're ever likely to meet. After dropping out of her Fine Art course at Central St Martin's she started wielding the needle in 1997, a long process of watching and learning, she says. She set up Shangri-La in 2005 and specialises in traditional Japanese designs merged with a contemporary graphic aesthetic. While tattoos have become more socially acceptable and fashionable, she shuns fluorescents (she's dubious about their safety) in favour of using three or four colours, harking back to an era when tattoo art from the east met with western influences. Many people come in to the parlour with their own design and as it's such a personal thing, Lesley encourages people to make a few visits to discuss their designs and generally feel comfortable with the whole process.

Fashion//

Map 1
No.28

Shangri-La
52 Kingsland Road
E2 8DP

T: 020 7739 3066

www.lesleychan.
com

Open/
11am-6pm,
Mon-Sat

Map 1
No.29

Squint
3 Redchurch Street
E2 7DJ

T: 020 7739 9275

www.squintlimited.
com

Open/
11am-6pm,
Wed-Fri;
11am-5pm, Sat

Squint

Shunning anything bland, Lisa Whatmough turns antique sofas and modern classics into something fresh with bold creativity. She has a design relationship with Liberty, where her pieces have been sold for a couple of years now and been invited to dress up parts of the store. With her new boutique, she is concentrating on commissions. Anyone wanting a traditional chaise longue re-upholstered with brightly patterned textiles should pay a visit. The attention to traditional craftsmanship is matched by her commitment to sourcing original quality pieces of furniture or updating those that customer have brought in, ripe for reinvention – her stint working in antiques helped refine her sourcing skills. But it's a return to her roots in fine art that show through in her work, where a couch becomes a feast for eyes as much as a comfort for the behind.

Today is Boring

A friendly DVD hire shop run by friendly locals Adam and Tree Carr (local by way of Canada and the US). Film fans, they set up the shop in 2003 seeing a gap in the market for a decent video shop that isn't full of the usual Hollywood rubbish. You can search the broad collection of art-house, experimental, world and classic cinema by leafing through one of the catalogues, which aren't just organised by genre, but also mood, so if you're feeling groggy grab the 'what's good to watch while hung-over' folder. Their special events are more than just screenings, torch-lit choral events for The Night Porter and a 36-hour Twin Peaks marathon being just a couple of tasters of membership privileges.

Entertain-ment//

**Map 1
No.30**

Today is Boring
15 Kingsland Road
E2 8AA

T: 020 7684 1461

www.
todayisboring.com

Open/
3pm-11pm,
every day

Two Columbia
Road
2 Columbia Road
E2 7NN

T: 020 7729 9933

www.
twocolumbia
road.com

Open/
Noon-7pm,
Tues-Fri;
noon-6pm, Sat;
10am-3pm, Sun

Two Columbia Road

Owner Keith Roberts promises he only sells pieces of furniture he likes, and if you share his taste for classic, modernist Scandinavian furniture you're on to a winner. He goes on regular forays to Europe to track down more original and reconditioned pieces and is often asked to kit out bars, such as Milk & Honey in Soho, so desks from designers such as Hans Wegner often don't hang around for long. As well as the sleek classics, there's decent turnover in art, some from the local BritArt crowd of Tracey Emin and Gilbert and George as well as the likes of John and Sylvia Reid. There's also one of Ronnie Kray's daubs painted while in the clink. Keith's dad owned seminal 1960s boutique Mr Freedom and has inherited a nose for the quirky – he recently had a model bi-plane and some stuffed bird in the shop.

Unto This Last

Funny name for a furniture shop, you might think. It comes from the title of John Ruskin's 1860 book that advocated the return to local craftsmanship at the height of the industrial revolution. This nineteenth-century artisan spirit has combined with modern computer aided design and manufacture techniques to produce a range of furniture made solely from laminated plywood, mostly birch from sustainable forests in Latvia. This gives the simple design of the pieces, from fruit bowls to shelves and beds, a unique aesthetic and a contemporary look. It's all made on the premises using computer controlled equipment and 3D modelling software; you can watch the robots do their thing from behind a glass screen. As well as boasting the ability to make more or less any piece of furniture to size within a week, the shop/workshop also has numerous ready to buy pieces, our favourites being the beautifully curvy Nurbs coffee table (£580) and Spline chair (£200).

Unto This Last
230 Brick Lane
E2

T: 020 7613 0882

www.untothislast.
co.uk

Open/
10am-6pm,
every day

La Viande
3 Charlotte Road
EC2A 3DH

T: 020 7613 0988

www.laviande.
co.uk

Open/
Check website for
opening times

La Viande

A relatively new addition to the Hoxton art scene, La Viande was opened by Loughborough art college graduate Ellen Cumber in 2005. The two floors of the grand fire engine red Victorian building are given over to rolling exhibitions of the big four: painting, illustration, photography and sculpture. Ellen also hires out the space, but is aiming to curate more exhibitions by her own supported young contemporary artists. The unusual name is a reference to a family history of meat – the Cumbers have been farmers and butchers from Berkshire since the seventeenth century. With an eclectic and open-minded approach to contemporary art, who's to say some chops and cutlets won't make an appearance as part of an exhibition some day?

Wawa

This area is home to a wealth of designer-makers, who Wawa (aka Richard Ward) has been steadily promoting alongside his own range of sofas. His personal route to being a sofa designer and manufacturer began when he tired for working in the film industry and went back to something more akin to his roots in sculpture. The showroom around the corner from Columbia Road was his sculpture studio, before the sofa biz really took off. Now it's home to numerous examples of his modern interpretations of fairly classic designs, with a focus on bold colours and unfussy lines. Space constraints has meant that they are no longer manufactured on the premises, but are still made locally. Lucy Wassell's rugs , Helen Rawlinson's lamps and Mat Fothergill's leather handbags add to the growing range of interior design and fashion products you might also go ga-ga for.

Wawa
3 Ezra Street
E2 7HR

T: 020 7729 6768

www.wawa.co.uk

Open/
10am-2.30pm Sun;
by appointment on
other days

Search and
Destroy
1 Cheshire Street
E2 6EH

T; 020 7613 5604

Open/
Noon-8pm
Mon-Sat;
11am-6pm, Sun

www.
searchanddestroy.
co.uk

Search and Destroy

In its previous incarnation as City
16, Seach and Destroy had cutting-
edge digital designers and artists
as neighbours, but they didn't do
much for sales. So they upped-
sticks and moved from Shoreditch's
Charlotte Street to this prime position
just off Brick Lane in the summer
of 2006, changing their moniker
in the process. New vinyl is the
mainstay, most of it dance-oriented,
encompassing everything from
tech-house to electro. Only trance
or handbag house DJs will find no
room at the inn. There's more than
records here though. Owner Jerry
is a student of football history and
the shop's book selection covers
the subject as well as other tomes
on popular culture and modern
political philosophy. This might
make it sound like a bit of a bloke-
heavy environment, but the range
of fashion magazines and books,
brings in the girls - not that such a
cosmopolitan area as Brick Lane
adheres to such gender stereotypes
you understand.

in·de·pend·ent

free from the
authority, control,
or domination
of somebody or
something else,
especially not
controlled by
another state or
organization and
able to self-govern

Map 2

interesting venue
cafe
pub
market
wi-fi
restaurants
museum
underground
overground

Middle Lane

Lane

Park Road

Choai Cafe

Florians

Tottenham

Weston Park

The Broadway

Crouch Hall Road

Highgate

Kings Head

Hornsey Library

Satay Malasia

Crouch End Hill

Crouch Hill

100m

Buses: W7, W5, 91, 41. **Tube:** Nearest tubes Highgate (15 minute walk), Finsbury Park (take W7 bus) or Archway (take 41 bus).

What's There/

Internet/wireless(wi/fi): Paying internet access at Fotoplus, 3 Park Road, N8 8TE. Free internet and wi/fi at Hornsey library, Haringey Park, N8 9JA. **Cafes:** Sable d'Or Patisserie, 43 The Broadway, Crouch End, N8 8DT, World café, 130 Crouch Hill, N8 9DY, Pick More Daisies, 12 Crouch End Hill, N8 8AA. **Pubs:** King's Head, 2 Crouch End Hill, N8 8AA, Florians, 4 Topsfield Parade, Middle Lane, N8 8PR. **Restaurants:** Aanya's, 29 Park Road, N8 8TE, Khoai Café, 6 Topsfield Parade, Middle Lane, N8 8PR , Satay Malaysia, 10 Crouch End Hill, N8 8AA. **Market:** None in Crouch End but there's a nearby Sunday farmer's market at Alexandra Palace (www.alexandrapalace.com). **Parks:** Priory Park, Stationers Park. **Book shops:** Oxfam bookshop 22 Park Road, Crouch End London N8 8TD

Crouch End

During the Middle Ages, Crouch End was a small hamlet on land belonging to the Bishop of London. Centuries later the invention of the railways led to rapid urbanisation of the area, and Crouch End laid claim to its own station in 1867. As the population grew, so did its middle class population, and by the end of the 19th century The Broadway shopping area was open for business. Much of Crouch End, now a relaxed, upmarket playground for young professionals and families, is a conservation area. Shoppers still head for The Broadway and its adjoining streets, which are lined with bars, restaurants and quirky shops and boutiques. The famous Crouch End clock tower stands at its centre, inscribed in honour of Henry Reader Wiliams Esq, a local wine-merchant who saved nearby Highgate Woods from development. Quietly cool, compact and community-led, Crouch End may be one of London's harder-to-reach shopping hubs, but it's well worth the effort.

Powder
5 Topsfield Parade,
London N8 8PR,

T:020 8347 4100

Open/
9.30am-6pm,
Mon-Fri;
9.30am-6.30pm;
Sat,
Noon-4pm, Sun

Powder

The place to go for your designer fix, boutique Powder is home to a catwalk of big names; Diane von Furstenburg, Paul & Joe, Gharani Strok and Cacharel. Smaller designers such as Metallicus and Little Gem jewellery have their fair share of shelf space, and owner Sarah Curren (who also heads up www.mywardrobe.com) regularly stocks up with new finds from fashion forays to Milan and Paris. Whether you're after a simple jeans-and-t combo (Sass & Bide or Rogan from £120, C&C bell neck tops from £52) or a bit more glamour (DVF red paisley silk wrap jersey dress £278), something in the Powder wardrobe should please. A recent refurb has given the shop a fresh, Japanese-inspired contemporary look, pairing lacquer units with gentle greens, golds and reds for a minimalist, feminine feel.

Prospero Books

A potter round Prospero is a welcome antidote to the high-street book chains. There's no Starbucks corner, no free wi-fi and no novelty calendars; just plenty of pristine volumes, packed into dark wooden shelves and stacked up in piles upon the floor. Prospero has a well-worn feel, and its slightly musty smell will take you right back to the early excitement of the children's library. It's worth hanging about if you fancy bumping into a Crouch End literary celebrity – John Pilger is a regular browser – and the shop also has an impressive array of local interest books and maps.

Prospero Books
32 The Broadway,
London
N8 9SU

T: 020 8444 7588

Open/
9.30am-6pm
Mon-Sat,
11am-5pm, Sun

Map 2
No.3

Italian Foodhall
26 The Broadway,
Crouch End
London
N8 9DE

T: 02083476065 /
02083478673

Open/
8am-9pm Mon-Sat;
Sun, closed

Italian Foodhall

If the urge to escape London has gripped you but it's still only Monday, follow the whiff of freshly-brewed Italian coffee to the door of the Italian Foodhall. With its string of small outdoor tables lining a small grass square, the Foodhall brings a touch of al fresco café culture to Crouch End. Inside, the diner-deli throngs with buggy-pushers grabbing a home-cooked takeaway or sitting down at a banquette for a traditional Sicilian meal; chicken escalope with pasta and salad (£6.95), vegetarian lasagna (£6.50), or a large dollop of limoncello ice-cream (£3.50). While meal prices may be canteen-like, the food shelves rival those of Harrods, so transport yourself to Tuscany with a wander through the jumbo jars of sundried tomatoes, joints of prosciutto and boxes of Italian sweets.

Sally Bourne

Sally Bourne's interiors shop is a dangerous place. The moment you're lured inside, the urge to redecorate your home becomes almost irresistible. Specialising in antique furniture and accessories for house and garden, her eye for the stylish, the tasteful and the unusual makes for an eclectic mix. Each wall compartment holds a new treat - French fabric cushions, a pair of antique scales, or elegant ceramics by Sophie Cook - and the central table blooms with bunches of beautiful made fabric flowers. Her decor range from the practical (rolls of wipeable acrylic tablecloth linen (£18.99/metre)) to the downright fanciful (Scandinavian skis and tobaggans (from £150)). As well as supporting small designers, Sally is a trained potter herself, and sells her beautiful textured ceramic tiles from the shop's back room.

Home//

**Map 2
No.4**

Sally Bourne
10 Middle Lane,
London N8 8PL,

T:020 8340 3333
E:info@sallybourn
einteriors.co.uk

Open/
10am-6pm
Mon-Sat;
noon-6pm, Sun

Of Special Interest
42a- 46 Park Road,
London
N8 8TD

T:020 8340 0909

Open/
11am-6pm
Mon-Fri;
10am-6pm, Sat
noon-5pm, Sun

Of Special Interest

Of Special Interest feels more like a home than an interiors shop - a home you wouldn't mind adopting. Each of its four small rooms is laid out as if to be lived in. The first is a dining room where a beautiful antique wood table is laden with colourful crockery, delicate silk pot plants and wrought iron bowls of wooden fruit. Next door has a bright conservatory feel created by huge antique mirrors and set off by a glittering black crystal chandelier. The relaxed atmosphere comes also from the exuberant welcome of owners Belinda Bradley and Stephen Loftus, who have turned Of Special Interest into a Crouch End classic. Established in 1988, many shoppers are dedicated regulars, and Belinda and Stephen do their best to keep them interested, totally refurbishing the shop every season to show how the furniture and accessories can work in different ways. And if you don't find what you're looking for in the shop itself, ask for the key to their warehouse out back.

Form

Cool interior design store Form claims to be 'all about the customer', and if its incredibly helpful staff is anything to go by, they've probably got it right. Form is a great place to go if you're feeling decoratively uninspired. The small space is packed with quirky ideas, classic looks and everything in between for your bathroom, sitting room and kitchen, and the shop runs a bespoke design service to help you create your fantasy pad. Alongside new designers and second-hand vintage pieces sit some pretty big names; Louis Paulson and Verner Panton lighting, Charles Eames chairs, LSA glasswear and collectors' toys by Yoshitomo Nara. But you can find lights from £15, chairs from £20, as well as lots of smaller gifty bits and pieces.

Form
39 Park Road,
London N8 8TE

T: 020 8348 7080

Open/
10am-6.30pm
Mon-Sat,
noon-5.30pm, Sun

Joy
136 Crouch Hill,
London
N8 9DX

T: 020 8342 8020

Open/
10am-6pm
Mon-Sat,
noon-5pm Sun.

Joy

If you're in a girly mood or simply feel the need for some bodily pampering, Joy gives exactly what it says on the tin. Its sexy pink interior boasts shelf after shelf of skincare products and top-end toiletries, including ranges by Ren, Jurlique, Edward Coudray and Jean-Charles Brosseau. A backroom houses organic lines such as Dr Hauschka and Neal's Yard, and babies get a look in too with Earth Friendly Baby and Burts Baby Bee. The shop's a winner if you're looking for presents - you'll find soft, silky nightwear by Fairtrade range Eternal Woman Nightwear (from £15), delicate crochet bath slippers sewn with tiny pearls (£20), or rows of scented candles by Bougies la Francaise (from £10). And once you've shopped till you've dropped, you can complete the pampering experience at the Joy therapy rooms next door.

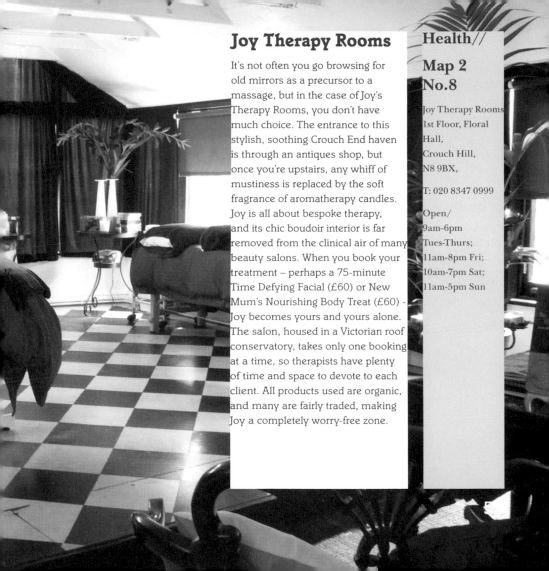

Joy Therapy Rooms

It's not often you go browsing for old mirrors as a precursor to a massage, but in the case of Joy's Therapy Rooms, you don't have much choice. The entrance to this stylish, soothing Crouch End haven is through an antiques shop, but once you're upstairs, any whiff of mustiness is replaced by the soft fragrance of aromatherapy candles. Joy is all about bespoke therapy, and its chic boudoir interior is far removed from the clinical air of many beauty salons. When you book your treatment – perhaps a 75-minute Time Defying Facial (£60) or New Mum's Nourishing Body Treat (£60) - Joy becomes yours and yours alone. The salon, housed in a Victorian roof conservatory, takes only one booking at a time, so therapists have plenty of time and space to devote to each client. All products used are organic, and many are fairly traded, making Joy a completely worry-free zone.

Joy Therapy Rooms
1st Floor, Floral Hall,
Crouch Hill,
N8 9BX,

T: 020 8347 0999

Open/
9am-6pm Tues-Thurs;
11am-8pm Fri;
10am-7pm Sat;
11am-5pm Sun

Coffee and Cake
28 Broadway
Parade,
London
N8 9DB

T: 020 8342 8989

Open/
8am-6pm,
Mon-Sun

Coffee and Cake

A large sign on the wall of gourmet traiteur, Coffee and Cake, reads 'Making bread is not work to me, it is a passion.' Signed by baker and proprietor, Ben Benammar, its sentiment is amply backed up by the baskets of crusty country loaves, fresh eggy cholla and soft chilli and corn bread that sit inside the shop's huge glass windows. The proof is also in the puddings – gooey chocolate cake, cream almond parcels and giant meringue swirls. The café's high white ceiling and exposed brick walls give it a fresh, modern feel and once you've indulged in breakfast it's tempting just to stay till lunch to sample Ben's summery British cuisine. The menu changes daily, featuring dishes such as crayfish on mango salad with lemon dressing (£7) and feta and spinach quiche with salad (£5.80).

glob·al·ise

to extend to
other or all parts
of the globe

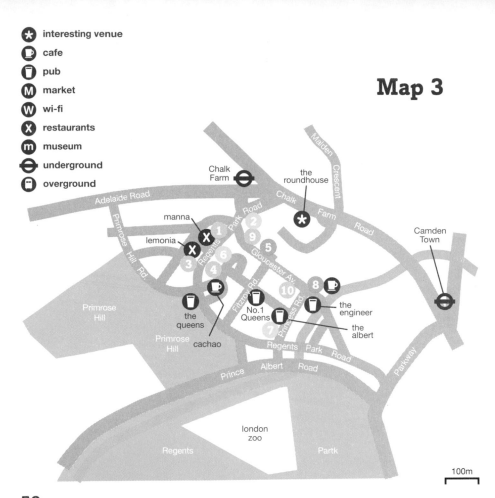

Map 3

Legend:
- interesting venue
- cafe
- pub
- market
- wi-fi
- restaurants
- museum
- underground
- overground

Chalk Farm

the roundhouse

Camden Town

Adelaide Road

Primrose Hill Rd

Park Road

Chalk Farm Road

Malden Crescent

manna

lemonia

1
2
9
5
6
4
3
10
8
7

Gloucester Av.

Fitzroy Rd.

Princess Rd.

the queens

cachao

No.1 Queens

the engineer

the albert

Primrose Hill

Primrose Hill

Regents

Prince Albert Road

Regents Park Road

Parkway

london zoo

Regents

Partk

100m

Nearest tube: Chalk Farm, Camden Town. **Buses:** 168, 274, C11

What's There/

Cafes: Troijka, 101 Regents Park Road; Primrose Pattiserie, 136 Regents Park Road; Cachao, 140 Regents Park Road **Pubs/bars:** The Albert,11 Princess Road; The Engineer, 65 Gloucester Ave; The Pembroke Castle, 150 Gloucester Ave; The Queens, 49 Regents Park Road. **Restaurants:** Lemonia, 89 Regents Park Road; Manna 4 Erskine Road. **Parks:** Primrose Hill, Regents Park

Culture/

Place of interest/local attraction: London Zoo, Regents Park Canal, The Roundhouse Theatre.

Primrose Hill

Fifteen years ago Primrose Hill was a tiny residential spot with a couple of Polish cafes, Greek restaurants, a Laundromat and a chip shop. With the arrival of cool Britannia in the 1990s, however, the area exploded. Actors, directors, designers and musicians flooded the Georgian houses in this sweet but central north London hamlet - from Jude Law and Sadie Frost to the Gallagher brothers. Primrose Hill got posh but it still managed to keep its sense of character, partly due to the small independent shops on Regents Park Road leading up the hill that refused to go mainstream. This area is a hot bed of independence as well as great for a dose of celeb spotting.

Beatrix Ong
117 Regents Park
Road
London NW1 8UR

T: 020 7449 0480
www.beatrixong.
com

Open/
10am-6pm,
Mon-Fri;
10am-6pm, Sat;
1-6pm, Sun

Beatrix Ong

Beatrix Ong is one of Britain best women's shoe designers – often touted as the next Jimmy Choo. This is the only place where you can find her full collection. The black interior is backed with four glass cases displaying pairs of vintage Ong shoes like artworks. Refreshingly, every kind of heel you could want is here from high stilettos to wedges to kitten heels to flip flops all made from supersoft Italian leather. The top seller is a daring patent red leather Mary Jane called Glare (£199) but this signature shoe comes in everything from python to matt black. A new range of bags with iPod holders and phone pockets is soon to arrive. And this store is also the only London stockists of Rrough-Rrough, rabbit fur lined dog carry bags that are -not surprisingly- very hot in LA.

Tann Rokka

Located in what was once Primrose Hill station on the bridge that leads over from Chalk Farm, the entrance to Tann Rokka is an alcove that leads to a long shop overflowing in antique and contemporary homewear. The name of the store is Romany (as in gypsy) for house talk, and people will be talking if you shop here. Many of the objects have oriental influences and are globally sourced, but art deco and even garden furniture line shelves. Tann Rokka also produces scented candles and a fragrance 'Kisu' with a sexy Japanese vibe. The shop has also collaborated with fashion designer Matthew Williamson (who lives locally) on a range of interiors fabrics and furniture – Tann Rokka can also give your own furniture a Williamson revamp.

Map 3 No.2

Tann Rokka
123 Regents
Park Road
NW1 8BE

T:020 7722 3999

www.tannrokka.
com

Open/
10am-6pm daily or
by appointment.

Studio 8
83 Regents Park Rd
London
NW1 8UY

T: 020 7449 0616

www.studio8uk.
com

Open/
10am-6pm,
Mon-Sat;
noon-5pm, Sun

Studio 8

This beautiful boutique settled on the shores of Primrose Hill a year ago. Studio 8 was originally started in South Africa a decade ago and still has branches in Cape Town and Johannesburg. The shop still maintains that international sense of style, selling womenswear with a fluid edge. The interior is all understated wood floors and Turkish rugs, but the bright accents of the coloured and graphic clothes spice things up. International labels include everything from Vivienne Westwood and Dosa to Sharon Guild and even bright polo shirts from Juicy Couture. Expect lots of loose knits, long dresses and linen aimed at a devoted clientele who like quirky unusual pieces in natural fabrics. The boutique jewellery is of special note. Alongside Masai bracelets made in Kenya there are stunning hand made African necklaces, designed by the South African poet Sue Clarke and made in the townships from cork covered in traditional prints.

Elias & Grace

This stunning mother and child store was opened in September 2005. It's a truly calming space – all white with a French feel to it. The children's clothes are for ages 0-5 with lots of classic cotton pieces from Belgian and French labels like Cacharel, Bonton and Petit Bateau. There's also lots of wooden kids toys and knitted sock monkeys for sale. Downstairs is a high end boutique for women. All the items are bought over a 9 month prosthetic bump so they work as maternity clothes but can work as 'normal' clothes. Expect an easy mix of high fashion labels with a beautifully chosen selection of Sonia Rykiel, Luella, See by Chloe, Matthew Williamson and Tocca interspersed with simple cotton layering by American Apparel and Humanoid Tees. There are also organic chemical free beauty products for during pregnancy. Don't be surprised if you bump into Sadie Frost or Kate Moss in the changing rooms...

Fashion//

Map 3
No.4

Elias & Grace
158 Regents Park
Road London
NW1 8XN

T: 020 7449 0574

www.
eliasandgrace.com

Open/
10am-6pm,
Mon-Sat;
12-6pm, Sun

The Lansdowne
90 Gloucester
Avenue
Primrose Hill
London
NW1 8HX

T: 020 7483 0409

Open/
6-11pm, Mon;
12-11pm, Tue-Sat;
12-10.30pm, Sun

The Landsdowne

Before The Lansdowne there were only pubs. This pioneering drinking establishment was one of the first gastropubs in London, sparking a trend that has taken over the country. Downstairs the high ceiling Victorian space is always busy with film, music and media types drinking beer or something from the very healthy selection of wines. The food served downstairs is rich, modern fare with international influences but a hearty pub vibe – fennel soups, smoked mackerel mains, plump chocolate puddings. The thin crust pizzas are especially popular. There's a full table service restaurant upstairs if you want something more intimate. It's a rare night when you don't spot someone famous in this pub ranging from Ross from Friends to Sadie Frost, but what makes the pub so cool is no one bats an eyelid.

Clifton

Eclectic style is de rigeur in Clifton interiors. This treasure trove of modern homewear brims objects high on unusual texture and design. Classic 20th century modernism sits next to international hand made crafts. There's everything from degree student ceramics and hand blown Venetian glass vases to vintage Arce lamps and 1960s tables. They have quite a lot of modern Italian names for sale including Missoni pillows and Italian Prandina lighting. If you're looking for something specific, Clifton also creates bespoke furniture pieces with their own joiners. There's also a selection of scarves and jewellery among the cushions and glass. Downstairs, Clifton has its own interior design firm in case the style of the store appeals so much you want them to do your whole house.

Home//

**Map 3
No.6**

Clifton
168 Regent's Park
Road
London
NW1 8XN

T: 020 7586 5533

www.
cliftoninteriors.
com

Open/
12-6pm, Mon-Fri;
12-5pm, Sat

**Map 3
No.7**

Maiden
9 Princess Road
Primrose Hill
London
NW1 8JR

T: 020 7449 0770

www.maiden-
uk.com

Open/
11am-7pm,
Tue-Sat,
12-5pm, Sun

Maiden

Calm and serene. These are the perfect words to describe this dream interiors shop in a residential street in Primrose Hill. Opened a year ago by stylist and interior designer Anna Unwin, the shop has every cream, beige, white, glass and stone piece you could ever want. There are handmade soaps, wooden cabinets, scented candles, leather armchairs, linen paintings and crockery made specifically for the shop by Brickett Davda. They even sell classic wooden nail brushes and functional old fashioned jars. The furniture is largely French and Swedish antiques that have been restored. They have a modern edge but are still full of worn charm. Not surprisingly, the celebrities that inhabit the area wander in a lot but Maiden also sells abroad a lot through their mail order service.

Melrose and Morgan

This glass fronted beacon of food fabulousness in Primrose Hill calls itself a grocery shop. It's a pretty low key name for a very high end independent store. Melrose and Morgan is a very special deli with an ultra modern interior. Inside every surface is covered in their specially made dishes – which they kindly deliver to your door. Their focus is on seasonal British produce and most items are largely organic. The food is proudly British (Eton mess, traditional cured British cheese, British juice like Chegworth). The shop also runs classic cooking classes and does catering for private events. In summer be sure to order (with 24 hours notice) one of their picnic hampers so you can dine with style on the nearby hill.

Food//

Map 3
No.8

Melrose
and Morgan
42 Gloucester
Avenue London
NW1 8JD

T: 020 7722 0011

www.melroseand
morgan.com

Open/
8am-8pm,
Tue-Fri,
8am-6pm Sat,
9am-6pm Sun

67

Miss Lala's
Boudoir
148 Gloucester Ave
Primrose Hill
London
NW1 8JA

T: 020 7483 1888

www.
misslalasboudoir.
co.uk

Open/
10am-6pm,
Mon-Wed, Fri-Sat;
10am-7pm Thur;
11am-5pm Sun

Miss Lala's Boudoir

It may only be a tiny one room shop, but Miss Lala's Boudoir literally overflows with all things frilly, flirty and fantastic. The shop specialises in lingerie by cult labels like Paris' Fifi Chachnil, Butchers and Snatch, Peachy Keen and Pistol Panties. Most of these items are handmade and very retro in style with lots of ruffles, chiffon and tie sides. Prices range from £12 for a pair of briefs to £150 sets. They also have special bridal pieces, 50s style dresses and some fun looking pink gingham maids outfits...The pretty pink shop also sells vintage jewellery, accessories including eel skin purses, scented candles and swimwear by labels like Roberto Cavalli. The shop was opened two years ago by Danish mother and daughter duo Mayanna and Fine Rees – who hire staff that could rival Agent Provacateur in the cute stakes.

Sweat Pea

Everything in Sioban O Neil's
jewellery shop in Primrose Hill
is displayed like a rare find. The
windows of this delightful blush pink
store are filled with glass domed
containers containing delicate gold
necklaces and earrings rather than
stuffed birds and animals. Inside
the shop stuffed owls, gilt mirrors
and a tree covered in black glitter
all decorate the room. The shop has
been open for four and half years
and has its own workshop with busy
designers downstairs. Every piece is
handmade, high fashion and has a
sense of delicate beauty. Most pieces
are made from 18 karat gold with
beads, precious and semi precious
stones. The results are feminine
without being twee. Sweet Pea also
guarantees something special and
unique that you simply won't find
anywhere else.

Fashion//

Map 3
No.10

Sweat Pea
77 Gloucester
Avenue
London
NW1 8LD

T:020 74499393

www.
sweetpeajewellery.
com

Open/
10am-6pm,
Mon-Sat

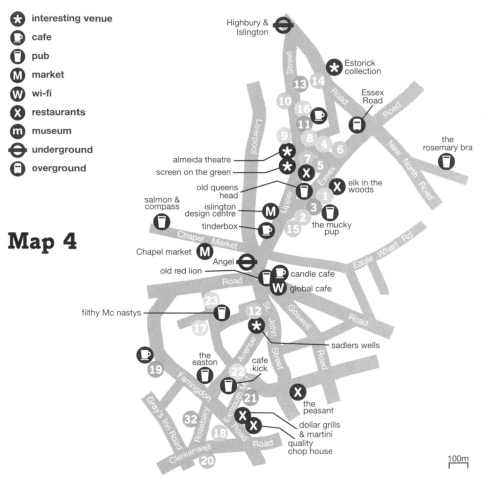

Map 4

Legend:
- interesting venue
- cafe
- pub
- market
- wi-fi
- restaurants
- museum
- underground
- overground

Highbury & Islington

Estorick collection

Essex Road

the rosemary bra

almeida theatre

screen on the green

old queens head

salmon & compass

islington design centre

elk in the woods

tinderbox

the mucky pup

Chapel market

Angel

old red lion

candle cafe

global cafe

filthy Mc nastys

sadlers wells

the easton

cafe kick

the peasant

dollar grills & martini

quality chop house

100m

Angel Islington, Clerkenwell

Getting there/

Tubes: Farringdon, Old Street, Angel, Highbury & Islington. **Buses:** 38, 55 Oxford St, 67, 73, 149, 271, 274,

What's There/

Internet/wireless: Net Station, 307 Gray's Inn Road; Upper Street and Islington High Street wifi hotzone; The World Café, 394 St John's Street. Cafes: Candid Café, 33 Torrens Street; Tinderbox, 21 Upper Street Konstam; Myddleton's café, Amwell Street. **Pubs/bars:** Old Queens Head, 44 Essex Road; Salmon and Compasses, 58 Penton St; Filthy McNastys, 68 Amwell St; The Old Red Lion Theatre & Pub, 418 St Johns St; Café Kick, 43 Exmouth Market; the mucky pup (dog friendly pub), 39 Queens head st; the Rosemary Branch (pub/theatre), 2 Shepperton Road, N1; the Easton (gastro pub), Easton st. N1. **Restaurants:** Almeida, 30 Almeida St; The Elk in the Woods, 37 Camden Passage; Afghan Kitchen, 39 Islington Green; Pasha (Turkish), 301 Upper Street. Quality Chop House, 94 Farringdon Road; Peasant, 240 St John Street; Dollar Grills & Martini, 2 Exmouth Market. Markets: Chapel Market [Tue-Sun]; Camden Passage [Wed+Sat];

Culture/

Festivals: Angel Canal Festival September. **Place of interest:** Screen on the Green (independent cinema), 83 Upper street. **Museums/galleries:** Sadlers Wells, Roseberry Ave; The Almeida Theatre, Almeida street; Estorick Collection of Modern Italian Art, Canonbury Square; Barbican Centre, Silk Street; Charles Dickens Museum, 48 Dougherty Street; Museum of London, London Wall. **Parks:** Highbury Fields; Gray's Inn Gardens; Bunhill Fields

Despite Angel's large number of big name behemoths on Upper Street, the area has still managed to keep some independent gems. At the same time other areas have kept their urban grit – like Chapel Market and spots towards Highbury. It's this combination that makes Islington so inviting. Clerkenwell's roots as a meeting place for radical political groups can be hard to see for the designers and media types that populate this hip area by day and the clubbers heading to Fabric by night. Go to Exmouth Mkt. for some of the best places to shop and stop to eat.

Hygge
35 Camden
Passage
Islington
London
N1 8EA

T: 020 7704 8633

www.hygge-life.
co.uk

Open/
11am-6pm,
Tue-Wed;
11am-7pm Thur;
10am-6pm, Sat;
12-5pm Sun

Hygge

Hygge is the Danish word to describe a convivial, cosy feeling. The items in this delightful Scando interiors shop certainly create that emotion. This large cream shop in Camden Passage is full of unique homewear. Open for nearly a year, there are lots of quirky items like "dirty" and "dishy" tea towels, ceramic brooches, burnt wood place mats and handmade, stitched lace teacup holders. Alongside the fun small items like birdhouses and wooden toys, there are also beautiful larger pieces like an £880 chair upholstered in thick cream argyle knit and bold graphic screenprints. Everything feels very natural here – like the items you'd find in a fairy tale cottage in Finland that happened to be created by cutting edge designers.

KiMantra

If you want a dose of lunchtime rejuvenation, KiMantra is for you. This affordable health and beauty stop has transformed an old antique shop in Camden Passage into a modern space with massage rooms, beauty rooms and a juice bar. Downstairs is red and black, with a bar selling juices like the 'Mokito' of lemon, lime, apple and mint. (They even have a juice delivery service to local offices). KiMantra also sell MBT's infamous cellulite busting shoes, and organic beauty products including Burts Bees and gems like fennel toothpaste. Treatments upstairs include a fast 15 minute head and back massage for £10, as well as your usual facials and waxing (for men and women). If you want something hardcore they have hot stones massage or Ki mantra yogic massage at £65 for an hour. Or go all out luxury and get the two hour Chavutti-Thai massage with oil, feet and ropes.

Health//

Map 4
No.2

KiMantra
5 Camden Passage
Islington
London
N1 8EU

T: 020 7226 8860

www.kimantra.com

OPen 12-8pm,
Mon; 10-8pm, Tue-
Sat; 10-6pm, Sun

Paul A Young
33 camden passage
Islington
London
N1 8EA

T: 020 7424 5750

www.payoung.net

Open/
11am-6pm,
Tue-Wed,
Fri-Sat;
11am-8pm Thur;
12-5pm Sun

Paul A Young

Paul A Young has been called the Heston Blumenthal of chocolate. The award winning chocolate chef worked with Marco Pierre White as a pastry chef at The Criterion Brasserie and later Quo Vadis, before becoming a consultant on chocolate for Harrods and Charbonnel. His eponymous shop has been open for only a few months, but has already gained international press attention as the most innovative chocolate shop in the world. It's also the most delicious. All the chocolates, brownies, macarrons and cakes are made on site and there are little plates with tasters to dive into around the shop. Alongside classics expect the unexpected – including purple violet, sea salted caramel and iridescent marmite chocolates. Alongside his own handmade truffles are pure chocolate sourced like fine wines from around the globe. He also facilitates chocolate workshops if you want to do it all yourself.

Fandango

If the idea of travelling across Europe to fill a van with vintage furniture feels like too much hard work, let Fandango do it for you. The 'urban antique' shop has a stunning selection of furniture, ceramics, artworks and glasswear sourced across the continent. Items range from Danish ceramic lamps to Art deco Belgian relief sculptures and ultra collectible Eames chairs. French 1940s café mirrors sit next to lights sourced in Danish church halls. There's a workshop in back of the small store where they clean up and restore found objects. The shop's been open for 5 years and is happy to ship items abroad if desired. Be sure to keep an eye open for the shop's cat lazing in warm corners.

Map 4
No.4

Fandango
50 Cross Street
London
N1 2BA

T: 020 7226 1777

www.fandango.
uk.com

Open/
11am-6pm,
Tue-Sat;
by appt Sun-Mon

Loop
Knit Salon
41 Cross Street
London
N1 2BB

T: 020 7288 1160

www.loop.gb.com

Open/
11am-6pm,
Tue-Sat;
12-5pm, Sun

Loop

It's impossible not to fall in love with knitting after visiting Loop. This recently opened mecca for knitters is hidden in the more residential part of Cross Street. There's nowhere quite like it in the country. The narrow white interior filled with shelves laden with every colour and textured yarn you could imagine. The owners source their wools from around the world from Bolivia to Japan and include the wildest colours and textures including hand dyed silk, lurex, Alpaca cotton and classic Italian wool. Nothing is wrapped in plastic so you can touch and feel the yarn you choose. Other knitting and crocheting supplies include beautiful bags, with nooks for needles, books and zines on knitting, as well as knitted toys (from £16 to £75) and art objects made by London designers. They also hold knitting classes for beginners and children and a free drop in SOS clinic on Saturdays!

Susy Harper

British fashion designer Susy Harper opened her store on Cross street three years ago. The small boutique devoted to her eponymous label has the feel of a French atelier in Paris. All the clothes are all made onsite and the focus is on wearable but modern classics with lots of natural materials like cotton and linen. Expect loose knits in deep rust and purple, as well as more tailored military influence macs. The designer's emphasis is on simplicity but with interesting shapes and textures to make it feel modern. The store itself is very simple with a granite floor and white walls decorated with candelabras a subtle showcase for the clothes. The handmade jewellery is also of note – expect lovely bright beaded necklaces and cut perspex brooches with a pop vibe.

Fashion//

Map 4
No.6

Susy Harper
44 Cross Street
London
N1 2BA

T: 020 7288 0820

Open/
11am-6pm, Tue-
Sat; 12-5pm, Sun

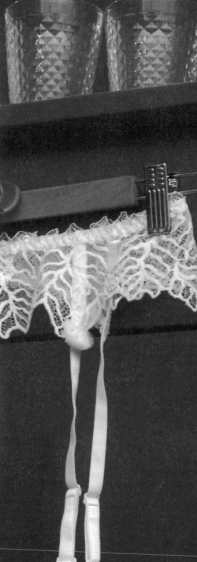

Tallulah Lingerie
65 Cross Street
Islington
London
N1 2BB

T: 020 7704 0066

www.tallulah-
lingerie.co.uk

Open/
12.30-4pm, Mon;
11am-6.30pm,
Tue-Fri;
10.30am-6.30pm,
Sat;
12.30-5pm, Sun

Tallulah Lingerie

Entering the red boudoir interior of Tallulah Lingerie is a lovely contrast to the bustle of nearby Upper Street. The lingerie boutique stocks a fabulous wide range of international labels including Aubade, Lejaby, Huit, Wolford, Damaris, Glitter & Twisted and Elle McPherson. (Prices range from £28 to £130 for a bra, but the average set costs around £75). Owner Nicola Rance changes stock regularly but has kept one bestseller in supply since she opened the store in November 2003 - the original double strand pearl thong designed by Bracli Pearls... There's lots of decadent silks here too, including sleepwear, camisoles and even sleep masks embroidered with "Wake Me Up For Coffee". Tallulah also sells a great range of reversible bikinis from cult label Moontide. Customers range from 18 to 80, and the strict confidentiality policy of the store attracts a lot of celebrities with a penchant for decadence.

Tribe

Tribe was one of the driving stores pioneering a modern take on rugs. The shop was opened six years ago by fireman turned rug expert Derek Owen and his textile designer wife Rebecca Tyndall. The shop specialises in handmade, contemporary rugs with a very modern linear aesthetic. These pieces made in places like South Africa, Iran, Nepal, Afghanistan, Turkey, Tibet and Morocco all have a graphic simple style but employ the same classic techniques used for centuries. Most are hand woven and naturally dyed. The rugs range from £240 to £3000 and they have a full approval service allowing you to test drive the rugs in situ. Smaller budgets can also enjoy the selection of beautiful pillows including Kimono silk cushions designed by Peoni and Kuba cloth African cushions.

Home//

**Map 4
No.8**

Tribe
52 Cross Street
Islington
London
N1 2BA

T: 020 7226 5544

www.tribe-london.
com

Open/
11am-6pm,
Tue-Sat;
12-5pm, Sun

Map 4
No.9

Atelier Abigail
Ahern
137 Upper Street
Islington
London
N1 1QP

T: 020 7354 8181

www.atelierabigail
ahern.com

Open/
10am-6.30pm,
Mon-Sat;
12-5pm, Sun

Atelier Abigail Ahern

Formerly located on nearby Cross
Street, this modern interiors shop
has been on Upper Street since
September 2005. Begun by interior
designer and stylist Abigail Ahern,
the shop specialises in everything
beautiful for your home. Its like a
dinner party set all in one shop.
There are giant candles, fluffy
pillows, turquoise dinner plates,
hand stitched felted table mats
and Tunisian mouth blown glass
vases. The aesthetic is zen glamour,
with lots of pieces sourced in
Italy including the brilliant Rastas
- hand woven Italian pillows made
from lime Merino Wool (£450)
that resemble a mass of dreads.
Alongside the textiles, tablewear and
lighting, the store also sells vintage
furniture from France, Belgium and
Italy and contemporary artworks.
The shop also runs wedding lists for
couples with serious taste.

Labour of Love

Designer Francesca Forcolini opened this edgy boutique on Upper Street two and half year ago and its dragged even the coolest fashionistas out of Shoreditch. The black interior store filled with antique cabinets stocks the shops own label range of knitwear alongside jewels like TSE's diffusion line cashmere and experimental glamour from Aganovitch and Yung. There's also a great range of shoes ranging from pastel metallic ballet pumps to Eley Kishimoto pop art heels. The accessories are just as creative as the womenswear, with tables strewn with vintage sunglasses, leopard print parasols, cut mirror butterfly brooches, handmade graphic purses, gold lobster claw pendants by Benedicte and cross stitch badges. There's even old fashioned floral tea cups – so you can sit down and relax after spreeing on clothes.

Fashion//

Map 4
No.10

Labour of Love
193 Upper Street
London
N1 1RQ

T: 020 73549333

www.labour-of-love.co.uk

Open/
11am-6.30pm
Mon-Wed, Fri;
11am-7.30pm
Thur;
10am-6.30pm Sat;
Noon-5.30 Sun

Map 4
No.11

Ottolenghi
287 Upper Street
London
N1 2TZ

T: 020 7288 1454

www.ottolenghi.
co.uk

Open/
8am-11pm
Mon-Sat,
9am-7pm Sun

Ottolenghi

The interior of designer deli Ottolenghi almost looks like a Stanley Kubrick film set – but with salads and cakes. The futuristic white space is based around a long white communal table reached by passing homemade breads and piles of roasted aubergine with saffron yoghurt, pistachios and basil. The food is truly stupendous – brimming with flavour, day bought ingredients and seriously good preparation. Expect mains like smoked haddock and organic salmon fishcake with a roasted chilli and tomato sauce. The food is almost too good to be English. Even the croissants are made fresh with French flour and butter. The shop has branches in Kensington and Notting Hill, but the Angel store is the real pull for lazy weekends with the papers. They also sell salads, quiches and cakes as takeaway and have a private catering menu if you want to take the whole experience home.

Saloon

Saddle up and get yourself to Saloon where Keiko Hindley has been selling an eclectic mix of fashion for men and women for the last four years to the well styled of North London. The aim is to provide accessible clothing that can't be found on the high street, but without being wilfully wacky or avant garde. Designers from London, Paris, Finland and Japan are among the mix, including the cool styling of Peter Jensen and the marvellously named Ivana Helsinki. Bags and jewellery complement the fashion accessories, plus a selection of homewear from 1960s Finish design studio Marimekko. Their classic textile prints can be found on cushions and other homely ephemera.

Fashion//

Map 4
No.12

Saloon
23 Arlington Way
EC1R 1UY

T: 020 7278 4497

www.saloonshop.
co.uk

Open/
11am-7pm,
Mon, Wed- Fri;
11am-6pm, Tues;
Noon-6pm Sat

Monte's
23 Canonbury
Lane
London
N1

T: 020 7354 4335

www.montesdeli.
com

Open/
10am-7pm
Mon-Fri,
10am-6pm Sat,
10.30am-4pm Sun

Monte's

Who ever said music was the food of
love didn't wander into this delicious
deli on Canonbury Lane. The purple
space lit by vibrant UV is a den of
delights. The food is largely sourced
in Italy and breathes continental
authenticity. If antipasti and sauces
are your thing, there are bowls
brimming with melezane pesto,
Boscaiola Olives and Cipollini (baby
onions). There's a great array of
cheeses like sweet Pecorino Dolce
and Etorki made with sheep milk,
and salami and sausages. Monte's
also sells giant jars of readymade
treats like cassolette as well as
jams, pickles and chutneys that are
attractive enough to give as gifts.
This family business, which has been
running for 11 years, also create
made to order hampers if you want
to go all out. There's even bottles
of Chianti, Prosecco or Illy coffee if
you want something to wash it all
down with.

Palette

This amazing fashion boutique brims with vintage gems from some of the best designers of the 20th and 21st century. The main draw is the womenswear. The shop stocks high-end designs from lesser known innovative contemporary labels alongside beautiful sourced vintage pieces by Missoni, Ossie Clark, Halston, Diane von Furstenburg, Chanel and Jean Muir. Even British Vogue has endorsed Palette as a must. There's also a great range of vintage shoes from the 1920s onwards and jewellery include Bakelite bangles and glass beaded necklaces. Interiors fans will like the carefully chosen modern furnishings in this den of delights, with unusual pieces by local artists like Barley Massey's tongue in cheek pop stools. The staff are delightful – and run a request service if you're looking for something specific.

Fashion//

Map 4
No.14

Palette
21 Canonbury
Lane
London
N1 2AS

T: 020 7288 7428

www.palette-
london.com

Open/
11am-6.30pm
Mon-Sat;
12-5.30pm, Sun

Lollipop
114 Islington
High Street
London
N1 8EG

T: 020 7226 4005

www.
lollipoplondon.
com

Open/
10 am-6pm
Mon - Tue
11am - 19:00,
Wed - Sat
10:00 - 17:00, S un

Lollipop

London may be one of the biggest cities in the world, but it's still bloody hard to find comfortable shoes that look beautiful. The butter soft leather numbers in this stunning Camden Passage shoe boutique are overwhelming comfortable. Shoes are carefully chosen from labels like Beatrix Ong and Buddahood to cover every heel height desired from wedge to flip flops. There are lots of unusual colour and shape variations - don't expect any bland black shoes here. Metallic red or blue grey suede are much more common. Lollipop also sells a great range of unusual coloured boots. Lollipop is seriously high fashion without the ego issues. Don't be surprised if you see girls with their noses pressed to the window each night dreaming of what to buy the next day.

Twentytwentyone

Twentytwentyone has been at the forefront of the modern penchant for minimalist contemporary design for over a decade. The upmarket shop has two branches in Angel – the original intimate store on Upper Street and the larger warehouse on nearby River Street. Both have become meccas for couples searching for the perfect Aalto chair on a weekend. There's a giant range of new and (near mint) vintage furniture and lighting here from seminal companies like Cappellini and Artek and by designers like Tom Dixon and Jean Marie Massaud. There's something for everyone hear – if the iconic Norman Cherner chairs are too expensive you can always settle for a fork or a piece of Ittala glasswear. Even toilet brushes look good in this home emporium.

Home//

Map 4 No.16

Twentytwentyone
274 Upper Street
London
N1 2UA

T: 020 7288 1996

www.
twentytwentyone.
com

Open/
10am-6pm,
Mon-Fri;
10am-5.30pm, Sat;
Noon-5pm Sun

Home//

Map 4
No.17

EC1
65 Amwell Street
EC1R 1UR

T: 020 7833 9669

www.ec1lighting.
co.uk

Open/
10am -5pm,
Mon-Sat

EC1

From their bijou premises not too far from King's Cross John Tunbridge offers an illuminating service to brighten your home. As a lighting contractor he supplies designers and architects, as well as homes and gardens for the general public, with contemporary lighting that suits every need. Up lighting, down lighting, wall-mounted, EC1 can do it. There's an emphasis on contemporary Italian companies among the suppliers, such as Foscarini, Oluce and Lumina. Within the shop itself are numerous lamp and shades, one of our recent favourites being a suspended lampshade made of old red glass soda bottles.

Best

Is this the best shop ever? It could be if you like new design, art and clothing that will either make you laugh, look good or feel a bit cooler than you really are. Or you'll think it's all a bit silly and too cool for school. Once you step inside, you'll be unsurprised to learn that much of the clothing and gifts are designed by young designers and artists, or that this store is on the same street as Central St Martin's School of Art. It all fits together in a happy atmosphere of hip designer t-shirts, gonzo-published mags and books on pop culture ephemera and slightly wacky home-made cards and presents - gems from artist David Shrigley feature among them. Also exhibited on the wall are works from hip young gun slingers on the London art scene, be it graff or mixed-media.

Fashion//

Map 4
No.18

Best
5 Back Hill
EC1R 5EN

T: 020 7833 5544

www.bestshopever.com

Open/
10am-7pm,
Mon- Fri;
11am -4pm, Sat

**Map 4
No.19**

109 King's Cross
Road
WC1X 9LR

T: 020 7833 2615

www.konstam.
co.uk

Open/
7.30am-4.30pm,
Mon - Fri;
8.30am-4.30pm,
Sat;
9am-4.30pm, Sun

Konstam

Oliver Rowe's café is a gem and worth travelling to. The former chef of Moro on Exmouth Market has produced a brilliant little place serving low-key food in a big way. There's no fuss over the sandwiches and breakfasts served until midday, just quality ingredients prepared with care. The take away salad boxes are great too, and seasonal. However, it's best to linger for lunch (served until 4pm), choose from a daily changing menu that could include char-grilled baby squid or courgette tomato frittata, all reasonably priced. Take a pew next to on one of the three wooden trestle tables in the comfortable and effortlessly stylish interior. A smoked glass mirror covers one wall, while the other is a corkboard plastered with postcards and an enormous stag made out of drawing pins. Oliver's latest project up the road serves only food from within the M25, but Konstam (named after his great-grandfather) needs no gimmicks to get by.

Magma

Bubbling through the crusty, musty surface of traditional bookshops, Magma has emerged as a place where creative energies can find their outlet on their shelves. More than just a design and art bookshop, it has evolved over the years to feature t-shirts, specially commissioned posters as well as magazines. Founders Montse and Marc opened this store after their initial 2000 Earlham Street shop became too crammed for all the other activities and ideas they had. The large space in the middle of the shop provides a comfortable air where design slouches and firebrands alike can browse, buy or try to find their muse among the tomes and mags. A line of Magma products from slip-mats to curtains from old fire blankets are in the offing. Being square has never been so hip.

Entertainment//

Map 4
No.20

Magma
117 -119
Clerkenwell Road
EC1R 5BY

T; 020 7242 9503

www.magmabooks.
co.uk

Open/
10am-7pm,
Mon-Sat

Brindisa
32 Exmouth
Market
EC1R 4QE

T: 020 772 1600

www.brindisa.com

Open/
10am-6pm,
Mon-Sat

Brindisa

The word Brindisa is derived from the Spanish 'brindis' meaning to make a toast, and plenty of north Londoners have been doing just that of late in honour of this popular Spanish food shop, elevating it to win the Best Retailer award in the Observer Food Monthly awards 2006. It's a cornucopia of Spanish produce all imported from the varied regions of Spain. Oils, cheese, tinned fish and squid, sherry and of course ham. The importance of ham and its hand-carving in Spain shouldn't be underestimated and the tradition and skills needed to slice the finest Serrano is upheld by the staff at this Exmouth Market store. Replete in their blue pinnies, staff are always friendly and happy to talk about their seasonal produce and love of the mother country.

Family Tree

A riot of colour along Exmouth Market, Family Tree extends its boughs of design and fashion across a network of up and coming talent. Takako and her husband set up the shop in the summer of 2004 and together with friends (hence the name Family Tree) produced a range of items that covered anything from Takako's jewellery to crocheted baby hats - all very cute and charming. A graphic design graduate, Takako has recently extended her own input into the shop's stock to a range of lamps and Japanese rice paper lampshades. Ten Swedish Designers (the name of the design collective) also have a range of limited edition items for sale in the shop. Hand-made greetings cards from Eastern Europe and clocks made from traditional French camembert cheese boxes are other favourites.

Fashion//

Map 4
No.22

Family Tree
53 Exmouth
Market
EC12 4QL

T: 020 7278 1084

www.
familytreeshop.
co.uk

Open/
10am-6pm
Mon-Wed, Fri;
11am-7pm,
Thur;
11am-6pm, Sat

The Hairdressers
70 Amwell Street
EC1R 1UU

T: 020 7713 0515

www.
thehairdressers.
info

Open/
10.30am-7pm,
Mon-Sat

The Hairdressers

A recent addition to the London hairdressing scene, the Hairdressers are Guy and Clair, friends who used to work at Jack's in Soho until deciding to go it alone in early 2006. Bringing their cutting skills and a relaxed attitude, the salon has a suitably homely and personal feel with books on the shelves and only four chairs. Part of this attitude comes from Guy who when working from home at his Shoreditch loft noticed how much his clients used to like getting their hair done in that environment. With the basement rented out to a theatre and opera designer, there's also a creative frisson, especially as many of Guy and Clair's regulars come from the world of theatre and the arts.

en·vi·ron·ment

the conditions that surround people and affect the way they live

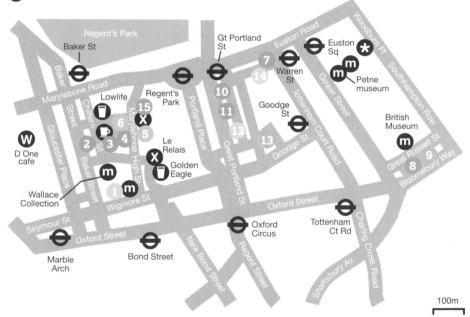

Map 5

- ✱ interesting venue
- 🍵 cafe
- 🍺 pub
- Ⓜ market
- Ⓦ wi-fi
- ✗ restaurants
- ⓜ museum
- ⊖ underground

Regent's Park

Baker St

Gt Portland St

Euston Road

Euston Sq

Woodburn Pl

Southampton Row

7

Warren St

14

Petrie museum

Marylebone Road

Chiltern St

Lowlife

Regent's Park

Portland Place

10

British Museum

Gower Street

Tottenham Court Road

Goodge St

Goodge St

11

12

13

8 9

Great Russell St

Bloomsbury Way

Ⓦ D One cafe

Gloucester Place

Baker Street

Marylebone High St

15

6

X

2 3 4 5

Le Relais

X

Golden Eagle

Great Portland St

ⓜ

ⓜ

1

Wallace Collection

Wigmore St

Oxford Street

Oxford Circus

Tottenham Ct Rd

Charing Cross Road

Seymour St

Oxford Street

Marble Arch

Bond Street

New Bond Street

Regent Street

Shaftsbury Av

100m

96

Getting There/
Tube: Bond St, Baker St, Oxford Circus; Tottenham Ct Road

What's There/
Internet/wi-fi: UK Explorer, 27 Melcombe Street; D One Café, Crawford Street ; Easy Internet Café, Tottenham Court Road. **Cafes:** Café Bagatelle at the Wallace Collection; Quiet Revolution – for chi-chi organic delights, 29 Marylebone High Street; Salumeria Dino, 15 Charlotte Place. **Pubs/bars:** Lowlife on Paddington Street for cocktails and DJ sets; Golden Eagle, a great traditional boozer, 59 Marylebone Lane; Fitzroy Tavern, 16 Charlotte Street; Nordic, 25 Newman Street; Angel, 61 St Giles High Street; Na Zdrowie, 11 Little Turnstile. **Restaurants:** La Fromagerie; Le Relais de Venise, 120 Marylebone Lane; Rasa Samudra, 5 Rathbone Street –good Keralan cuisine; Indian YMCA, 41 Fitzroy Square – amazingly cheap Indian food; Fino, 33 Charlotte Street. Markets: Marylebone Farmers Market is on Sundays

Culture/
Festivals: Marylebone festival, June. **Place of interest:** Chiltern street for Bridal wear. Sherlock Holmes museum, top of Baker street. Bloomsbury bowling underneath Tavistock Hotel, Tavistock Place; Pied Bull Yard, vintage camera shops. **Museums/galleries:** Grant Museum, UCL, Gower st. Wc1, Petrie Museum, Egyptian Archaeology, Malet Pl., Wc1, Percival David Foundation of Chinese Art, Gordon square, Wc1.Wigmore Hall for classical music – 36 Wigmore Street. Wallace Collection, Manchester Square. British Museum, Great Russell St, Wc1; Grant Museum; Parks:Regent's Park and Hyde Park; Fitzroy Square; Bedford Square; Russell Square Gardens.

Marylebone, Bloomsbury Fitzrovia

Get away from Oxford Street. Walk up Marylebone Lane to Marylebone High Street, where the area retains most of its 'villagey' charm among the Georgian townhouses. Bloomsbury famous for its host of academic institutions, the British Museum and an intellectual playground for the 'Bloomsbury Set' during the first half of the 20th century. It hasn't lost its Georgian charm, but duck away from Tottenham Court Road and Oxford Street towards Fitzroy Square and it has been spiced up by a new world of interesting shops, bars, cafés and restaurants.

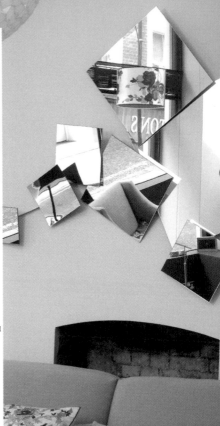

Mint
70 Wigmore Street
W1U 2SF

T: 020 722 4 4406

www.mintshop.
co.uk

Open/
10.30am- 6.30pm,
Mon-Wed,
Fri and Sat;
10.30am- 7.30pm,
Sun

Mint

John Martin curates this shop, which at first glance appears a rather sleek, yet bland interiors showroom. A closer look reveals a surprising mix of styles and pieces that if they don't liven up your life, will at least look rather lovely in your house. From lighting and candles to ceramics and decorative furniture, pieces are sourced by John from established designer companies such as Fontana to young design graduates fresh from end of year shows. A 200 year-old Greek mosaic might be sitting next to a stylised tray designed by a St Martin's graduate. While an eye for the interesting is all that's necessary to get Mint-ed, prices to start from the very affordable to the, well, if you have to ask you can't afford it.

Caroline Groves

Literally the place where dreams become reality, if your dreams are a pair of cashmere and suede orange and pink slingbacks that is. Caroline Groves offers a bespoke handmade shoe service – one of only a handful left in London. She will happily sit down with you to discuss and sketch out what you want during the consultation process – three or four are the norm –while taking detailed measurements and photographs of your feet and suggesting materials and sourcing the right leathers. Recalling the artisan spirit in her skilled handcrafting Caroline injects real passion into her shoes, making the experience a real pleasure. The styles are reminiscent of anything from 1920s to the 1950s recalling the glamour and nostalgia of the ear, while retaining a Noughties chic and elegance so you can step out in jaw-dropping style.

Fashion//

Map 5 No.2

Caroline Groves
37 Chiltern Street
W1U 7PW

T:020 7935 2329

www.
carolinegroves.
co.uk

La Fromagerie

La Fromagerie
2-4 Moxon Street
W1U 4EW

T:020 7935 0341

www.lafromagerie.
co.uk

Open/
10.30am-6pm,Mon
9am- 6pm,
Tues- Fri;
9am -7pm, Sat;
10am -6pm Sun

Great truckles of cheese are proudly displayed in the window, a statement of intent about the importance of fromage in this rather posh Marylebone deli. You see, while cheese is the word, and French cheese the speciality, there is more to La Fromagerie. Tidy shelves in the airy shop front are precisely stacked with all manner of preserves, olive oils and fresh fruit and vegetables. If you can't wait to get home head to a slightly raised area at the back underneath a skylight where delicacies can be enjoyed for lunch. Staff are incredibly well mannered. The 'cheeseroom' though could be the coolest place in the city, where seasonal, yes seasonal cheeses, sourced from small independent producers from the Pyrennese to Devon rest in a perfectly climate controlled environment throughout the year.

The Ginger Pig

The success of this esteemed butcher was actually a bit of a mistake; Timothy Wilson bought a disused farmhouse in Nottinghamshire and decided the adjacent barn looked a bit empty so bought three saddleback pigs for it. From these small piglets a mighty fine butchers emerged, first with a butchers attached the barn, then a stand at Borough market and later this shop in Marylebone. Timothy's grandfather was a farmer and butcher so it's in his blood, but national awards - National Food Producer of the Year 2005 - and becoming a supplier to some of London's top restaurants including the River Café, were somewhat of a surprise from what began mainly as an exercise in sustainable farming. The meat is reared on his farm up in Levisham on the Yorkshire moors and if you're after quality meat reared responsibly, this is the place to come.

Food//

Map 5
No.4

The Ginger Pig
8 & 10 Moxton
Street
W1U 4EW

T: 020 7935 7788

Open/
8.30am-6pm,
Mon-Sat;
9am-3pm, Sun

Mallon & Taub
35D Marylebone
High Street
W1U 4QB

T: 020 7935 8200

www.
mallonandtaub.
com

Open/
10am -6.30pm,
Mon- Wed,
Fri and Sat;
10am -7pm, Thur;
Noon-6pm, Sun

Mallon & Taub

It's clear to see why Mallon & Taub provide the cool eyewear for the classy and starry of the capital. An optician with a boutique feel, the emphasis here is on adding some dash and fashion fun to what would normally be the slightly tedious event of finding a pair of glasses. The shop itself has as much style as the frames that are provided by a wide range of labels and designers such as Alain Mikli, Face a Face, Oliver Peoples, YSL and Dior among others. The idea came from shop owners Joan Mallon and Shanah Taub, both fully qualified optometrists, who wanted to combine their love of fashion and shopping with their professional skill and create an experience that was as fun as buying as pair of shoes. With one-to-one service and helpful staff they do just that.

Public Image

Public Image has been servicing the heads of Marylebone for the past 25 years, and when owner Barry Cresswell isn't off for a break in Ibiza he's running the salon and charming the mix of locals and regulars. He worked with Trevor Sorbie and the salon offers a bit more fun and edge that many of the staid salons of the area with it's rich red interior and quirky, shabby chic décor. A skylight illuminates the four chairs where the five staff provide cuts, colours and dispense advice for those who just don't know what to do with their mop. Downstairs Claudia Fallah runs a beauty clinic with her own range of products, where those in search of truth in beauty can undergo anything from acid peels to manicures in search of that elusive ideal.

Map 5 No.6

Public Image
63 Paddington Street
W1U 4JF

T: 020 7935 0699

Open/
10am-7pm, Mon-Thur;
10am-8pm, Fri;
9am-5pm, Sun

Stern's World Café
75 Warren Street
W1T 5PF

T: 020 7387 2255

Open/
9am-6.30pm,
Mon-Fri;
11am-6.30pm, Sat

Stern's World Café

Stern's World Café does for world music and coffee what Ray's Jazz shop does for jazz now that it inhabits the first floor space of Foyles bookshop. Instead of beatnik hipsters sipping some java while listening to some free jazz, Stern's World clientele can opt for a range of coffee from across the globe (not just on Stern's own label) while buying the latest Bulgarian balalaika music or something from Femi Kuti's back catalogue. The racks of music inhabit the rear of the alarmingly orange shop and are organised by country of origin. Any indigenous folk counts as world music, so the US is represented by Nashville country. The bench seat opposite the counter of the café section stretches from one end of the shop to the other; apt then that it's upholstered in giraffe print material.

Camera Café

If you're a desperate wannabe and are having trouble getting into the tabloids, head to the Camera Café where members of the paparazzi often come to fuel up on caffeine before hitting the streets. But don't let this put you off. This snug café is tucked at the back of a camera sales shop, although the photography element was a later edition to the original café set up by Adrian Tang and his photography mad brother. The front counter has piles of photography equipment for sale, particularly Nikon and Leica models, and the limited space means thing pile up very quickly. Push through past the snappers and there's a small space for wi-fi access and some tables where coffee, cake or a cup of tea from the extensive menu can be enjoyed. If you'd prefer a longer exposure here, there's a 'function room' and comforting oriental food is also available.

Food//

Map 5
No.8

Camera Café
44 Museum Street
WC1A 1LY

T: 020 7831 1566

www.cameracafe
.co.uk

Open/
11am-7pm,
Mon-Fri;
noon-7pm, Sat

Bladerubber
12 Bury Place
WC1A 2JA

T:020 7831 4123

www.bladerubber.
co.uk

Open/
10.30am - 6pm,
Mon -Sat

Blade Rubber

A shop devoted to the humble rubber stamp? Yes, it is a little odd, but where else will you find a rubber stamp in London, and there are literally thousands of them stacked on the shelves here. What started as a stall at Greenwich crafts market developed into this haven for traditional ink and stamp lovers everywhere ten years ago. From simple shapes and whimsy to the more bizarre and humorous, there seems to be a stamp for every occasion, especially Christmas - the busiest time of the year - with customers wanting to make cheap and easy personalised cards. There is also a service to make up a stamp with your own personal design, which proves to be popular. The basement houses other arts and crafts equipment and is also the site for the shop run classes on card making and stamping techniques.

Jamie Aston

Flowers//

Map 5
No.10

Jamie Aston
226 Great Portland
Street
W1W 5AA

T: 020 7387 0999

www.jamieaston
.com

Jamie Aston is the Christian Dior of florists and probably the hippest in London. With an attention to arranging that a milliner gives to his clothing, Jamie and his team create floral works for art for any occasion from weddings and bar mitzvahs to catwalk shows. Fancy a Venetian theme to an event or garden party? No problem, the creative team can accommodate for any sized spectacular with their typical elegance. However if you're stuck for a Valentine's Day pressie, Jamie and his staff will happily help you out, steering absent-minded boyfriends and husbands away from the traditional red roses to something more dramatic, and appreciated. Jamie also runs classes from his 'school' -from one day, to two weeks -where enthusiastic beginners or even establish florists can catch up on the latest trends.

Villandry

Villandry
170 Great Portland
Street
W1W 5QB

T: 020 7631 3131

www.villandry.com

Open/
7.30am-10pm,
Mon-Sat;
9am-4pm, Sun

What started as a shabby, but happy little place on Marylebone High Street in 1989 now fills this voluminous space on Great Portland Street, with not only a food shop, but a 100-seater restaurant and next door a bar. It's a gourmand's heaven where the delight in good food hasn't been diluted by the large premises. The shop's bakers toil through the night to bring fresh bread, made only with organic wheat, to the shop shelves and the charcuterie and cheese counters are stocked with the finest European produce. What it lacks in small-scale intimacy, it makes up for in its range and the consistency of the quality of the food. It really is more than just a place to do posh grocery shopping, with the Charcuterie Bar next to the counter providing plates, light dinners and wine for those who like to linger, and a take away service available for those that don't.

Noel Hennessy

Striking out on his own in 1997 has paid dividends for Noel Hennessy. The relaxed atmosphere in the shop is in stark contrast to the slightly frosty and intimidating air of many contemporary furniture stores. A smartly attired chap himself, often sporting a bow-tie, his taste ranges from the modern and minimal designs of Spanish design house Nuevo Linea to the cool sophistication of Italian company Acerbis. As well as featuring furniture from British, Scandinavian and other European designers, there are pieces to cover every room in the house, apart from the kitchen, and a full interior design service is offered to customers – no space too small, no budget too big. With a complementary approach to lighting, a beautifully crafted piece from Mr Hennessy's shop can illuminate any home.

Home//

Map 5 No.12

Noel Hennessy
67A Great
Titchfield Street
W1W 7PT

T: 020 7323 3360

www.noelhennessy.
com

Open/
10am- 6pm,
Mon- Fri;
10am – 4.30pm,
Sat

Map 5
No.13

Teamwork
41-42 Foley Street
W1W 7JN

T: 020 7323 6455

www.
teamworkphoto
.com

Open/
9am-5.30pm,
Mon-Fri

Teamwork

A camera shop staffed by a crack team who know the business and cater for pros and amateurs that can tell their Leicas from their Hasselblads. Not that they aren't accommodating to those just getting to grips with photography, but one thing they don't do is deal with compact digitals. Three years ago they made to decision to focus on digital, but still supply anything - bodies, lens, paper – for 5x4 format. With great confidence they claim they can get anything a customer is after. Chromakey paint for green-screens? No, problem. And if it's not to be found among the wealth of accessories and lighting equipment already in the store, they can track it down through their extensive network of contacts. Short training courses are also available for digital camera photography, usually monthly, depending on demand.

Thorsten van Elten

Get any thoughts of Scandinavian furniture style and interior design out of your head. Thorsten van Elten doesn't do Scandi. The pieces of furniture, fun and innovative lighting and homeware that are self-branded come from Dutch, German, British and Czech designers and makers – the unifying principle being they are things he likes. The line in traditional tin toy cars and trains has a lovely retro look and perhaps unsurprisingly hails from the Czech Republic. The pigeon shaped light might make you coo and the giant tea cup plant pot illustrates a similarly subtle twist on homeware that would brighten any contemporary home. Thorsten himself comes from an interior design background and later worked as a buyer for shop, SCP. While he is doing less design of products himself, he is always on the look out to commission.

Home//

Map 5
No.14

Thorsten van Elten
22 Warren Street
W1T 5LU

T:020 7388 8008

www.thorstenvan
elten.com

Open/
10.30am-6.30pm,
Mon- Fri;
10.30am-6pm Sat

Rococo Chocolates
45 Marylebone
High Street
W1U 5HG

T: 020 7935 7780

www.
rococochocolates
.com

Open/
10am-6.30pm,
Mon- Sat;
11am-4pm, Sun

Rococo Chocolates

Chantal Coady has been pushing the boundaries of chocolate for the last 23 years. After opening her first store on Kings Road armed with little more than a passion for chocolate and a little business acumen she has expanded to this Marylebone shop and to a new chocolate factory in West Norwood. Hold the Willie Wonka fantasy, Chantal and her two fellow chocolatiers make all the delicious goodies themselves. Her recipes are always innovative and her ingredients of the highest quality. While there is a range of beautifully presented English fondants and truffles, choco lovers can also indulge in organic artisan bars, such as earl grey, cardamom and sea salt. Whatever your take on the emotional effects of chocolate, Rococo's delights will suit your every mood and give you a lift.

com·mu·ni·ty

a group of people
with a common
background or
with shared
interests within

Map 6

Legend:
- ⓧ interesting venue
- 🅟 cafe
- 🅟 pub
- Ⓜ market
- Ⓦ wi-fi
- Ⓧ restaurants
- ⓜ museum
- ⊖ underground
- ⊟ overground

Oxford Circus

Oxford Street

New Oxford St

Tottenham Court Road

Soho Sq

Great Marlborough Street

Poland St

Berwick St

Wardour Street

Dean Street

Frith Street

Greek Street

Charing Cross Road

Bar Italia

Endell St

Shaftsbury Avenue

Neal St

Covent Garden

Upper St Martin's Lane

Long Acre

Kingly Street

Regent Street

Carnaby Street

Broadwick Street

Lexington Street

Blue Post

Patisserie Valerie

Old Compton Street

French House

Beak Street

Brewer Street

Shaftsbury Avenue

Leicester Square

Piccadilly Circus

100m

Getting there/

Nearest tubes: Oxford Circus; Tottenham Court Road; Leicester Square; Piccadilly Circus

What's There/

Internet/wireless (wi-fi) point: There is planned blanket coverage in what is said to be Britains first wi-fi 'hotzone' a multi hotspot area offering blanket coverage. The zone stretches from the east end of Picadilly, through Picadilly Circus, down Coventry street as far as Wardour street. Of course many coffee shops in the area have wi-fi as well as Easy Internet Café, Tottenham Court Road; Netstream, 9-12 St. Annes Court, Soho 24 hrs. (internet, WiFi). **Cafes:** Bar Italia, 22 Frith Street; Carlton Coffee House, 41 Broadwick Street; Old Compton Café, Old Compton Street; Patisserie Valerie, Old Compton Street. **Pubs/bars:** Blue Posts, corner of Broadwick st. and Berwick st.; The Endurance, 90 Berwick Street; Bradley's Spanish Bar, 42 Hanway Street; The French House, 49 Dean Street. **Restaurants:** Yauatcha, 15 Broadwick Street (excellent Chinese) Mildred's, 45 Lexington Street. Hakkasan, 8 Hanway Place; Red Fort, 77 Dean Street; St Moritz, 161 Wardour Street. There's also the whole of Chinatown to choose from.

Culture/

Festivals/Events: Gay Pride, first Saturday in July. www.pridelondon.org. Museums/galleries: The British Museum, Great Russell Street; Grant Museum; Percival David Collection, 53 Gordon Square; Petrie Museum, Malet Place; Opera House, Covent Garden.
Parks: Soho Square, great place to people watch on a sunny lunchtime.

Soho, Carnaby Street, Covent Garden

If you can't find what you want here, it doesn't exist. The beating heart of London's shopping and entertainment district stretches from the square mile of Soho to the calmer reaches of theatre land in Covent Garden. There are boutiques around the fringes of Carnaby Street where the importance of fashion is still as strong as it was in the 1960s and 70s. People watching in Soho is often as much fun as shopping. The myriad of cafes, restaurants and bars, should sate any ardent shopper's appetite.

Tatty Devine
57B Brewer Street
W1F 9EL

T: 020 7434 2257

www.tattydevine.
com

Open/
11am-7pm,
Mon-Sat

Tatty Devine

Shabby chic? Not quite. Unusual costume style jewellery and fashion accessories for those who want something a bit different from this increasingly hip label. What started seven years ago as an idea by Rosie and Harriet, two painting graduates from Chelsea School of Art, has blossomed into an internationally renowned operation. As well as this store in Soho and the original one in Brick Lane, Tatty Devine's fun and pretty things are now stocked in around 100 boutiques across the globe. But keeping things individual and unique is still the aim. Using materials from wood to plastic acrylic, all the jewellery is designed in-house and made at the Brick Lane studio using a laser cutter. With some pieces being quite nostalgic with a twist of modern design, to more out there items, there should be something wonderfully tatty for everyone.

Sister Ray

Selectadisc is dead, long live Sister Ray! Not so much a Soho record shop putsch as a taking over of premises, Sister Ray moved up to the larger space on Berwick Street when Selectadisc went to the big vinyl press in the sky. From humble beginnings as a stall in Camden Market in the mid-1980s, Sister Ray has grown up to be one of London's foremost alternative vinyl and CD suppliers of anything from stadium rock to nose-bleed techno white labels. The extensive back catalogue of rock and indie fills racks that wrap around the edges of the front part of the shop. More selective and niche genres can be found deeper in the store. Recognising the fact that vinyl is far from dead owner Phil Barton is keen to supply as many 12in records and rarities as possible, an ethos that should please both DJs and collectors of the big old discs.

Sister Ray
34 Berwick Street
W1F 0UF

T: 020 7734 3297

www.sisterray.co.uk

Open/
9.30am- 8pm,
Mon-Sat;
noon-6pm, Sun

Hip Hop   UK Hip Hop

Perpetuity
69 Neal Street
WC2H

T: 020 7240 7666

www.perpetuity.biz

Open/
11am-6.30pm
Mon-Wed,
Fri and Sat;
11am-7pm, Sat

Perpetuity

Michael Gordon was a photographer and Ricci Stoene was a stylist. Having worked in and around the fashion industry for years, in early 2005 they decided to dive into making jewellery themselves. Perpetuity aims to be cutting edge but without the steep price tag attached to so many boutique jewellers. The quality of the design is high with both Michael and Ricci, plus one other, designing the jewellery themselves. There's a focus on men's pieces, from bracelets to watches as well as some shiny things for women, including earrings and rings. Marmite jars with silver lids are a fun addition to the collection that is regularly added to. Other great gifts including the most bling iPod covers you could hope for crafted from silver, gold or platinum.

Lina's Stores

One of Jamie Oliver's favourite Italian delis lies in the heart of west Soho Lina's has been selling the finest Italian produce and homemade pasta for yonks and has attracted a loyal local following and a gathering glut of foodies from further afield. The interior is testament to the authenticity of the place – it's free of any style make-overs, and if there are wooden crates full of aubergines on display, it's because they arrived like that. It remains charmingly old fashioned with the range of imported Italian fare, from beans to porcini and olive oil stacked on the full-to-busting shelves. Homemade pasta and sausages are winners here.

Food//

**Map 6
No.4**

Lina's Stores
18 Brewer Street
W1R 3 FS

T: 020 7437 6482

Open/
8am-6.30pm,
Mon-Fri;
8am-5.30pm, Sat

Map 6 No.5

Freud
198 Shaftesbury
Avenue
WC2H 8JL

T: 020 7831 1071

www.freudliving.
co.uk

Open/
11am-7pm,
Mon-Fri;
11am-6pm, Sat;
11am-5pm, Sun

Freud

Freud has a simple style that will appeal to many and offend few. The in-house design team has created a range of homewear, the picks of which being the stainless steel coffee pots and champagne coolers and the hand-blown glass. Perhaps more interesting goods are the Charles Rennie Mackintosh furniture range. Faithful to his original drawings the tables and chairs can be made to order and are made with wood from sustainable sources. The large bowed front windows are the original Victorian ones. Should you purchase some polite homeware, Freud café and bar downstairs is a fine spot to sip a cocktail (margartias could be better) and check out the exhibition of the month on the walls.

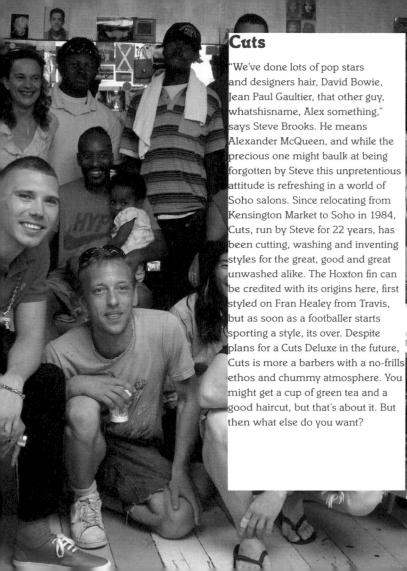

Cuts

"We've done lots of pop stars and designers hair, David Bowie, Jean Paul Gaultier, that other guy, whatshisname, Alex something," says Steve Brooks. He means Alexander McQueen, and while the precious one might baulk at being forgotten by Steve this unpretentious attitude is refreshing in a world of Soho salons. Since relocating from Kensington Market to Soho in 1984, Cuts, run by Steve for 22 years, has been cutting, washing and inventing styles for the great, good and great unwashed alike. The Hoxton fin can be credited with its origins here, first styled on Fran Healey from Travis, but as soon as a footballer starts sporting a style, its over. Despite plans for a Cuts Deluxe in the future, Cuts is more a barbers with a no-frills ethos and chummy atmosphere. You might get a cup of green tea and a good haircut, but that's about it. But then what else do you want?

Cuts
39 Frith Street
W1D 5LL
T: 020 7734 2171

Open/
11am-7pm,
Mon- Sat;
noon-5pm Sun

**Map 6
No.7**

Play Lounge
19 Beak Street
W1P 9RF

T:020 7287 7073

www.playlounge.
com

Play Lounge

Toys aren't just for kids, OK. Some of us might still own our favourite toy from when we were little and then there are some of us that covert the latest set of In-Crowd figures from James Jarvis or some rare Japanese cult action figure as much as any consumer durable. Fun and good design are two of the keys to the oddities, toys, games, books and figures in the Playlounge and there are some great, silly things to be had – the latest wonderful adventures of Tony Millionaire's Sock Monkey and Drinky Crow and limited edition t-shirts designed by Pete Fowler to name just two. If that doesn't mean anything to you, don't worry, come down and play anyway.

Doors

Owned by bag designer Jas M.B, Doors is your portal to designer clothing and a great range of the successful Jas M. B slouchy-look leather bags. If you're a man about town you can find plenty here to look the part and also invest in that now much maligned item the man bag, although you might not want to call it that. Manager and buyer for the men's wear that makes up most of the stock, Keven McDermott, has a keen eye for new season trends and up and coming young designers. He keeps things rolling by often having different designer's collections in store depending on the season. Recently Doors has been the exclusive London stockist for creations by Marios and Dioniso.

Entertain-
ment//

Map 6
No.8

Doors
8 Ganton Street
W1F 7PQ

T: 020 7494 2288

www.
doorsbyjasmb.com

Open/
11am-7pm,
Mon-Sat;
noon- 5pm, Sun

SKK Ltd
34 Lexington
Street
W1F 0LH

T: 020 7434 4095

www.skk.ne

Open/
10am-6.30pm,
Mon-Fri;
11am-6.30, Sat

SKK Ltd.

Terence Conran is lighting architect
Shui Kay Kan's nemesis. While
Conran was dictating what everyone
should buy through Habitat, Shui
moved to London from Hong Kong
and had enough faith left in the great
unwashed to let the them decide. His
philosophy then is more democratic,
working with his team to design
and manufacture a wide range of
lighting and is unafraid of returning
to the drawing board if something
doesn't sell. He's far from beholden
to the customer's wallet, but his
fun and innovative designs, such
as his inflatable Christmas trees,
plastic moulded gorilla and Buddha
lights have been huge hits. He's
accumulated a range of corporate
clients over the past 16 years, from
lighting Liberty's diamond jewellery
to kitting out a Moscow nightclub.
With a keen eye on the world's
energy problems, he's developing
lighting using energy efficient LEDs,
utilising all their creative possibilities.

Twinkled

Was it an accident that the last four digits of Twinkled phone number of 1978? They're incredibly apt for this emporium of retro and kitsch has such a wealth of goods from the last few decades of the twentieth century that you could happily live in a house that would have looked the height of style and good taste in that year. From tiki-style mini bars to plastic pineapple-shaped ice buckets you could live it up in your front room sipping a martini like a vintage Roger Moore. The range of men's and women's clothing is extensive so there's no worries about not looking the part (if they haven't got a safari suit in store, they'll keep an eye out for one for you). The authentic items really do cover everything for the vintage metropolitan lifestyle, including all that stuff most of us are glad we got rid of all those years ago – framed oil portrait of a poodle anyone?

Fashion//

Map 6
No.10

Twinkled
15 Kingley Court
Carnaby Street
W1b 5PW

T: 020 7734 1978

www.twinkled.net

Open/
11am-7pm,
Mon-Wed, Sat;
11am-8pm,
Thur, Fri;
noon-6pm, Sun

Map 6
No.11

Beyond the Valley
2 Newburgh Street
W1F 7RD

T: 020 7437 7338

www.
beyondthevalley.
com

Open/
11.30am-6.3pm,
Mon- Sat;
noon-5pm, Sun

Beyond the Valley

Jo, Kate and Kristjana graduated from Central St Martin's and had a plan to launch themselves and other new designers towards the lofty peaks of the art, fashion and design industries. Their store is a trove of new products, jewellery, illustration and other items all produced in limited quantities. Over 100 recent graduates from Central St Martin's, RCA and Goldsmith are featured in the store and in the online shop. There is also a clothing range under the moniker Beyond the Valley, but the store likes to think of it as a stepping stone for the art and design community as well, also offering itself as a studio and exhibition space.

Orla Kiely

Orla graduated from a master's degree at the Royal College of Art and surveyed the fashion scene in the 1990s. Despite the general trend towards the minimal and black, she wasn't going to join in. Even with a philosophy that holds function over form it didn't mean dull. Her first range of bold print design handbags have spawned a growing empire of her recognisable work the world over as well as two recent capsule collections for the Tate. This flagship store has a prime position just off Cambridge Circus and is home to a wide range of her bags and patterned items, all reflecting her own bright and optimistic spirit. From cushions to bags, buying into it a little pick-me-up for any girl about town.

Fashion//

Map 6
No.12

Orla Kiely
31 Monmouth
Street
WC2H 9DD

T: 020 7240 4022

www.orlakiely.com

Open/
10am-6pm,
Mon-Wed,
Fri and Sat;
10am-7pm, Thur;
11am-4pm, Sun

Two See
17 Monmouth
Street
WC2H 9DD

T: 020 7240 7692

www.twoseelife.
com

Open/
11am-7pm,
Mon-Sat;
1pm-6pm, Sun

Two See

A boutique that champions fashion with nine labels exclusive to the store. Anthony Stephinson is the manager and buyer whose taste for couture and style is reflected in the range of men's and women's wear. He's also guardian of the natty minibar by the counter where customers who share his passion can linger over a cocktail. Parisian designer Jean-Charles de Castelbajac dressed Madonna and other luminaries of the 1980s and 1990s, but until his latest season at Two See, hasn't been seen on these shores since. Patrik Rzepski's collection is not only exclusive to Two See in the UK, but also Europe. Swedish label Birfitt is also another coup for Anthony, and the revival of Dexter Wong's men's wear has proved popular with everyone from fashion students to geezers who wore his clothes in the 1980s. It's also the place to be for lavish opening nights and events, especially during London Fashion Week.

Coffee, Cake and Kink

Coffee, check. Cake, check. Dildos and erotica, check. A café that the likes of Dita von Teese would no doubt approve of, run by the hospitable and accommodating husband and wife team of Alan and Sonia Cassidy. Get any thoughts of sleazy Soho out of your head, this is a light and bright café, bookshop and gallery where you're encouraged to relax, chat or browse the erotica, toys and extras over a caffetier of coffee and a slice of cake. The philosophy behind it is more about being yourself than getting off, although Alan (author of the London fetish map) admits it was a project born out of a frustration at not being able to find a place to relax and meet like minded people. Whatever your pleasure might be, there might be something here for you – the red lounge downstairs hosts regular events - apart from cappuccinos, there'll be no froth here.

Food//

Map 6 No.14

Coffee, Cake and Kink
61 Endell Street
WC2H 9AJ

T: 020 7419 2996

www.coffeecake andkink.com

Open/
11am-8pm,
Mon-Thur, Sun;
11am-11pm,
Fri and Sat

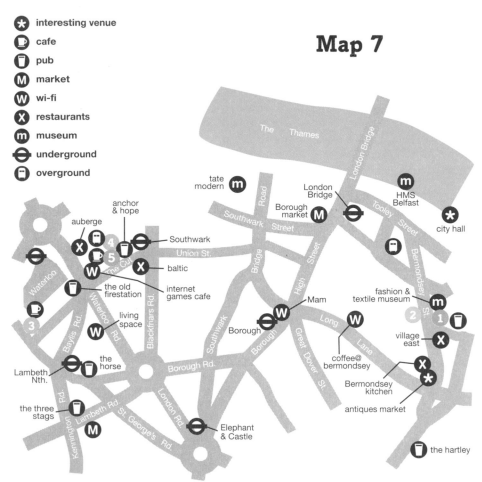

Map 7

Legend:

- ⊛ interesting venue
- ☕ cafe
- 🍺 pub
- Ⓜ market
- Ⓦ wi-fi
- Ⓧ restaurants
- ⓜ museum
- ⊖ underground
- ⊟ overground

The Thames

tate modern ⓜ

London Bridge

Borough market Ⓜ

ⓜ HMS Belfast

⊛ city hall

Tooley Street

anchor & hope

auberge

Ⓧ

4

☕ 5

Southwark

Union St.

Southwark Street

Southwark Bridge Road

High Street

London Bridge

Ⓦ The Cut

Ⓧ baltic

internet games cafe

the old firestation

Waterloo

Waterloo Rd.

Blackfriars Rd.

Ⓦ living space

Ⓦ Mam

Borough ⊖

Great Dover St.

Long Lane

Ⓦ

coffee@ bermondsey

fashion & textile museum ⓜ

Bermondsey St.

2

1 🍺

village east Ⓧ

Ⓧ Bermondsey kitchen

⊛ antiques market

Baylis Rd.

☕

3

the horse 🍺

Lambeth Nth. ⊖

Borough Rd.

Southwark Bridge Road

London Road

the three stags 🍺

Lambeth Rd.

Kennington Rd.

St. George's Rd.

Ⓜ

Elephant & Castle ⊖

🍺 the hartley

Getting There/

Buses: 21, C10, 40, 35. Tube: Bermondsey; London Bridge. **Rail:** London Bridge. Boat: London Bridge City Pier

What's There/

Internet: Cafe @ Bermondsey Indoor Antiques Market 247 Long Lane SE1; Mam Internet Cafe & Coffee Bar 282-302 Borough High Street London; Living Space, 1 Coral Street; Internet Games Café, 117 Waterloo Road. **Cafes:** Design Museum Café, 28 Shad Thames SE1; Film Café, National Film Theatre, South Bank. Restaurants: Auberge, 1 Sandell Street SE1; Baltic, 74 Blackfriars Road; Village East, 171-173 Bermondsey St; Bermondsey Kitchen, 194 Bermondsey Street; Auberge, 1 Sandell Street; Baltic, 74 Blackfriars Road. Pubs: The Hartley, 64 Tower Bridge Road; Anchor and Hope, 36 The Cut; The Old Fire Station, 149 Waterloo Road; The Horse, 124 Westminster Bridge Road; The Three Stags, 67-69 Kennington Road. **Markets:** Bermondsey Road Antiques Market (Sundays, 6am-2pm) Borough Food Market (Saturdays) South Bank Book Market (Sundays). **Places of Interest:** City Hall, The Queen's Walk SE1; The London Aquarium, County Hall, Westminster Bridge Road; British Airways London Eye, County Hall; Royal Festival Hall, South Bank Centre.

Culture/

Museums/Galleries: Fashion and Textile Museum, 83 Bermondsey Street SE1 (currently closed); Design Museum, Shad Thames; HMS Belfast, Morgan's Lane, Tooley Street; Hayward Gallery, South Bank Centre; County Hall Gallery, County Hall; Tate Gallery, Bankside

Bermondsey, Waterloo

By the late 1800s Bermondsey was the hub of the capital's food processing industry – known as 'London's Larder' but fell into decline in the 1970s. Happily, the 1990s has seen major redevelopment. Head to Bermondsey Street and Tanner Street for the best of the area's boho hangouts. North of the station is the South Bank development – built in 1951 a colossal concrete monolith, housing the Royal Festival Hall, Hayward Gallery and the NFT. To the south, Lower Marsh Road offers a broad selection of hip vintage clothing shops and a nice mix of trendy and traditional local boozers.

131

The Garrison
99-101
Bermondsey St
SE1 3XB

T: 020 7089 9355

www.thegarrison.
co.uk

Open/
8am-11pm
Mon-Fri;
9am--11pm, Sat
9am-10.30pm, Sun

The Garrison

This elegant gastropub on the corner of Bermondsey Street is a testament to just how far this area has come in the last few years. It's not so long ago that Bermondsey was better known for brawling than for bars and bistros but your chances of seeing a scrap in this refined venue are about as high as your chances of being offered a stale cheese roll when you ask for the menu. The décor is text book shabby chic – all mismatched chairs and tables, squishy sofas and vintage lighting – and the food is equally considered with a menu boasting the likes of fois gras and roast guinea fowl. The clientele is comprised principally of young, style-conscious types who natter away convivially as they slurp down one of the ales or something from the impressive wine list. Downstairs is the cosy 'cinema room', which can be hired out for parties, screenings or just a footy match. Neat idea.

Cockfighter of Bermondsey

After successfully wholesaleing a limited range of eyecatching clothing, Cockfighter decided it was time to open its own boutique - and when the shop launched in November 2003 it was the only retail outlet on Bermondsey Street. Since then the brand has gone from strength to strength, extending the floor space and launching a new line in May 2006. Lucy Linden of Cockfighter proudly announces that the brand now attracts a remarkably diverse mix of customers comprising 'locals, musicians, fashionistas, artists and city boys' (mostly under the age of 30, we'll wager) - and it's no surprise when you look at the threads on offer. Their logo T-shirts and sweats, 50s-style bowling shirts and some pretty lurid dresses are just far enough away from mainstream to be trendy, but not so subversive they'll get you laughed at. A smattering of the new brand - Cock & Magpie - plus household names like Kangol and Havaiana complete the collection.

Fashion//

Map 7
No.2

Cockfighter of
Bermondsey
96 Bermondsey St
SE1 3UB

T: 020 7357 6482

www.cockfighter.
co.uk

Open/
11am-7pm
Tue-Fri
Noon-6pm, Sat
Mon by
appointments only

Scooterworks
132 Lower
Marsh Road
SE1 7AE

T: 020 7620 1421

www.scooterworks-
uk.com

Open/
10am-6pm,
Mon-Sat
Sun- closed or by
appointment

Scooterworks

If there's a cooler shop in the whole of London – or the world, for that matter – we've yet to find it. A showroom, workshop and café rolled into one, Scooterworks specializes in vintage Italian scooters. At the front of shop, 1960s Vespas line up alongside 1970s Lambrettas while at the back a huge Gaggia coffee machine burbles away approvingly while sharp young hipsters lounge around discussing the existentialist meanderings of Sartre and why a suit's side vents must never be more than five inches long. Probably.

The bugs on sale vary in condition from pristine to past it but, let's be honest, a Lambretta on its last legs has more style in its radiator column than a Harley has in the whole of its cumbersome chassis. If a scooter is a little bit precarious for you they'll also sell you the four wheel equivalent – a fiat 500 – or, for the truly laid back, how about vintage coffee machine? Be here now.

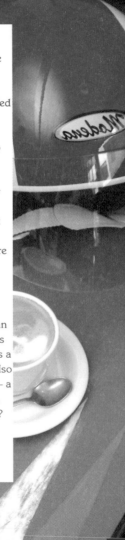

The London Bicycle Repair Shop

What do you expect from an establishment with a name like that? Well, bicycle repairs for a start – and you won't be disappointed. A dedicated team of mechanics can sort out pretty much any problem from a kerfuffle with your forks to a strain in your saddle – and the chaps are refreshingly down-to-earth and un-technical for bike geeks. But there's so much more to this cycling hub than maintenance. There's also a warehouse where they knock out new bikes – mainly mountain and hybrids – at lower prices than you'll find in the High Street, and they hire bikes if you're just after a bit of exercise on the weekend. Perhaps what marks this place out from the crowd most of all, though, is the cycling tours it organizes. For a modest fee they'll guide you round nine-mile routes through historic areas of East or West London. Does exactly what it says on the tin. And then some.

Entertainment//

Map 7
No.4

The London
Bicycle Repair
Shop
2/3 Benson House
SE1 8DQ

T:020 7928 6898

Open/
9am-6pm,
Mon- Fri
10am -4pm, Sat

Waterloo Sandwich
Bar
82 The Cut
SE1 8LW

T: 020 7922 1379

Open/
8.00am-4pm
Mon - Fri

Waterloo Sandwich Bar

Another Waterloo establishment with a solid, self-explanatory name. You'll find no la-di-da eateries with 'post-modern' monikers like 'crumpet' or 'egg' in this neck of the woods. Oh, no, just good honest traders like the London Bicycle Repair Shop, and this jolly sandwich bar. You may not be dazzled by the originality of the menu here – it's literally spuds, soups, salads and sandwiches – but what you will certainly appreciate is the friendliness of the service and the quality of the simple fare on offer. The Waterloo Sandwich Bar also has that most illusive – and essential – of qualities for a café – atmosphere. And it has it in spades. If the self-conscious cool of a joint like Scooterworks is a little too much for you, head down to The Cut for a nice cuppa and a good old chinwag.

ho·mog·e·nise

to become or
cause something
to become
homogeneous

Map 8

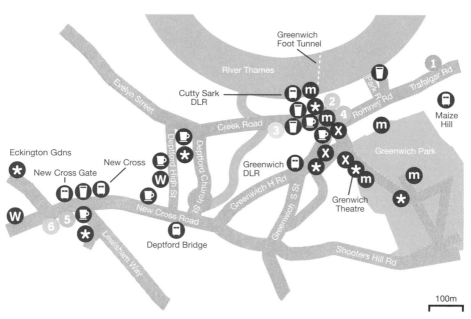

interesting venue
cafe
pub
market
wi-fi
restaurants
museum
underground

Greenwich Foot Tunnel

River Thames

Cutty Sark DLR

Creek Road

Evelyn Street

Deptford High St

Deptford Church St

Eckington Gdns

New Cross Gate

New Cross

New Cross Road

Greenwich DLR

Greenwich H Rd

Greenwich S St

Park Row Rd

Romney Rd

Trafalgar Rd

Maize Hill

Greenwich Park

Grenwich Theatre

Lewisham Way

Deptford Bridge

Shooters Hill Rd

100m

Getting There/

Buses: 172, 436, 36, 171, P13, 136 , 171, 225 , 53 / Greenwich 188, D7, 177, 286, 180, 177. **Tube:** New Cross, New Cross Gate, North Greenwich (Jubilee Line) **Rail:** New Cross, New Cross Gate, Greenwich. **DLR:** Cutty Sark. **Boat:** Westminster Pier

What's There/

Internet: Q T Internet Café, 160 New Cross Road; Dalsan Internet Cafe, 151 Deptford High St. **Cafes**: New Cross Café, 491 New Cross Road; Goddard's Pie House, 45 Greenwich Church Street; Pistachios 15 Nelson Rd. **Restaurants:** Thailand, 15 Lewisham Way; Elvis Gracelands Palace, 881-883 Old Kent Road [not on map];Rivington Restaurant, 180 Greenwich High Road; Bar Du Musee, 17 Nelson Road; Spread Eagle, 1-2 Stockwell Street. **Pubs:** Café Crema, 304 New Cross Road; The Walpole Arms, 407 New Cross Road; Admiral Hardy, 7 College Approach; Trafalgar Tavern, Park Row; Gypsy Moth, 60 Greenwich Church Street. **Market:** Greenwich Market (Thur-Sun)

Culture/

New Cross Broadway Theatre, 496 New Cross Road Greenwich Theatre, Crooms Hill. Greenwich Picture House, (independent cinema) 180 Greenwich High road. Festivals: Greenwich and Docklands International Festival (June). **Places of Interest:** Goldsmiths College; Greenwich Prime Meridian; Greenwich Foot Tunnel. Parks:Eckington Gardens; Greenwich Park. **Museums/ Galleries:** National Maritime Museum, Greenwich; Queen's House, Romney Road; Royal Observatory, Greenwich Park; Fan Museum, 12 Crooms Hill; Cutty Sark, King William Walk

Greenwich, New Cross

The New Cross Inn gave its name to a busy turnpike on the London to Dover Road. Today its around the students of Goldsmiths college that much of modern New Cross's boho vibe has sprung up. Deptford high st, is London before 'the clones' took grip, populated by an egg shop, fishmonger, gallery and two pie and mash shops. Greenwich one time favourite haunt of monarchs from Henry VIII to Victoria, is equal parts tourist hotspot and boho hangout. The centre has an appealingly relaxed, village-y feel that makes an afternoon's shopping more of a day out than an exhausting trawl.

Theatre of Wine
75 Trafalgar Road
London
SE10 9TS

T: 020 8858 6363

www.theatreof
wine.com

Open/
10am-9pm
Mon-Sat;
Noon-6pm, Sun

Theatre of Wine

Decanter magazine - the impeccably knowledgable wine industry publication - shortlisted Theatre of Wine for its Best Independent Wine Merchant Award in 2006 - so you can be sure these guys know their stuff. The shop opened in 2002 to meet demand in the gentrified area of Greenwich for a specialist wine merchant. Since then it has become an integral part of the local community - providing regular wine tastings and encouraging customers to engage in, and enjoy, what the owners describe as 'the wine experience'. Stock comprises a particularly strong collection of European wines - including rare champagnes and English sparkling wines - plus an array of unusual beers and fine spirits. The enthusiasm of the owners and staff is infectious - and is in no small part responsible for tremendous popularity of this classy, ecclectic merchant.

Johnny Rocket

Just a precious stone's throw from the riotous grotto of toys and games that is Compendia is this rather more modern, but equally unique outlet. Combining traditional techniques with cool, contemporary design Johnny Rocket has been making uber-hip jewellery and accessories for over 12 years. Having supplied items for legendary labels such as Gucci, Givenchy, Alexander McQueen and Julien MacDonald - not to mention counting Kylie, Fatboy Slim and Missy Elliot among his private clients - Johnny has a reputation unsurpassed in contemporary UK jewellery design. Working by commission in his own workshop the man himself can be engaged to create anything from diamond-set wedding rings to cufflinks - but be prepared to shell out a fair amount of cash for an original creation.

Fashion//

Map 8 No.2

Johnny Rocket
10 College
Approach
London
SE10 9HY

T: 020 8269 1814

www.johnny-rocket.co.uk

Open/
10am-6pm
Wed-Fri;
10am-5pm
Sat-Sun.
Appointments only
Mon-Tue

Map 8 No.3

Flying Duck
Enterprises
320-322 Creek
Road
London
SE10 9SW

T: 020 8858 1964

Open/
11am-6pm, Sat
10.30am-6.30pm
Sun;
Closed Mondays

Flying Duck

Step through the beaded curtain that hangs across the door of this South East London favourite and you'll discover a shady grotto crowded with all manner of retro delights. The interior is roughly split in two. In the explosion of brightly-coloured plastic and paper that occupies the space to the left of the door you'll find trendy toys and jokeshop novelties - from pens disguised as syringes to wind-up nun toys and pin badges declaring 'I love cock'. The right of the shop is reserved for deliciously kitsch homewares, lighting and accessories that range from the truly tacky (1970s top-shelf mags, anyone?) to the genuinely collectable - such as an original 1950s patterned tea set on a recent visit. Add to this a range of souvenirs dedicated to the King from 'Elvisly Yours' and you've got yourself a great big bag of thoroughly frivolous tricks. Or, as the shops own publicity puts it: 'Everything you want but don't need in your life'.

Compendia

Pick your way through the maze of small stalls stocked with antiques and handicrafts in the posh, covered section of Greenwich market and you'll find this eye-popping emporium of games and puzzles in one of the old retail units around the edge. Compendia is a real gem - packed floor to ceiling with games ancient and modern, familiar and rare. There's an exhaustive collection of board games - from old favourites like Risk and Rummikub to intriguing tactical challenges such as Carcassonne, in which the objective is to maintain control of a medieval French city - cool! You'll also find a great stock of card and dice games and puzzles. But the items that really catch the eye are classic wooden pub games like bagatelle shove ha'penny, and bar skittles. A truly rare find.

Entertain-
ment//

Map 8
No.4

Compendia
10 Greenwich
Market
London
SE10 9HZ

T: 020 8293 6616

www.compendia.
co.uk

Open/
11am-5.30pm
Seven days
a week

Entertain-
ment//

**Map 8
No.5**

Rubbish & Nasty
304 New Cross Rd
London
SE14 6AF

Open/
11am-7pm,
Mon-Fri;
1pm-6pm, Sat

Rubbish & Nasty

Ok, so it may be called "Rubbish & Nasty", and the combination of garish pink on a bottle green background on the shopfront may make the letters go all fuzzy in that way that leaves you feeling as though you're going to fall over, but don't let that put you off. Once inside, you'll discover everything in this curious store is a bit more welcoming. The laid-back atmosphere that pervades the shop is perfect for browsing its racks of records – which include no end of mind-boggling unsigned acts of the kind you only usually see on MySpace- and cool second hand clothes. Oh, and owners Ian and Sophie are a friendly couple as well. So not rubbish, and not at all nasty. Next door is the delightful Café Crema a hip hangout that stages regular screenings of arthouse and world cinema.

Prangsta

Stepping through the door of this delightful costumier is like stepping through the wardrobe in the Chronicles of Narnia. It's fantastic in every sense of the word, and some of the outfits available for hire or purchase are truly the stuff dreams are made of - or the stuff that's made up in dreams. Designed for anything from a fancy dress party to a full-on theatrical production, the costumes are divided into categories such as the 'Historical', 'Myths and Legends' and 'Uniforms'. Obviously it's a great place to head on Halloween, although, apparently, Burlesque is something of a speciality – which should stand them in good stead for the current craze for the ancient art of stripping. As well as being an oversized dressing-up box Prangsta also offers a wearable fashion range. The design retains a fanciful edge and has more than a touch of the Westwoods about it.

Fashion//

Map 8 No.6

Prangsta
304 New Cross Rd
London
SE14 6AF

T: 0208 694 9869

www.prangsta.
co.uk

Open/
11am-7pm,
Mon-Sat

Map 9

interesting venue
cafe
pub
market
wi-fi
restaurants
museum
underground
overground

Peckham Road

High St.

Peckham library

Clayton Rd.

Bellenden Rd.

Rye lane

Choumert Road

the wishing well

Dog Kennel Hill

East Dulwich

East Dulwich Rd.

Peckham Rye

Peckham Rye Common

Peckham Rye Park

Rye Forest

East Dulwich Grove

Lordship Lane

Barry Road

pavilion cafe

100m

What's There/

Internet: Southwark Public Library;
Ralph's Corner, 117 Dulwich Rd;
Dulwich Public library, Lordship
Lane. **Cafes:** Crossroads Café, 190
Bellenden Rd; Au Ciel, 1A Calton
Ave; Pavilion Café, Dulwich Park;
Blue Mountain Café, 18 Northcross
Rd. **Restaurants:** Peckham
Experiment, 168 Bellenden Rd;
Il Giardino, 7 Blenheim Grove;
Franklin's, 157 Lordship Lane;
Thai Corner Café, 44 Northcross
Rd. **Pubs:** Bar Story, 213 Blenheim
Grove; Palmerston, 91 Lordship
Lane; The Gowlett Arms, 62 Gowlett
Rd. **Markets:** Peckham Farmers
Market(Sun); Peckham St Market

Culture/

Festivals: I Love Peckham Festival
(Aug); Dulwich Festival (May)
Edward Alleyn Theatre, Dulwich
College, Dulwich Common; ED
Comedy at The Hob, 7 Devonshire
Rd. **Museums/Galleries:** Dulwich
Picture Gallery, Dulwich Village;
The Horniman Museum, 100
London Rd, Forest Hill.

Peckham, East Dulwich

With organizations like the Peckham Society and the loons who run ilovepeckham.com it obviously has a thriving community of locals who are proud of their neighbourhood and keen to enhance its reputation. The completion of the groundbreaking new library gave the area a nationally famous landmark and soon enough new shops, cafes and pubs started springing up as genuine gentrification began to take hold. Start on the High Street for a bit of bustle and investigate the side roads for a few cute local outlets. As hard to believe as it is now, Dulwich was once a rather poor relation to nearby Camberwell. These days, thanks in no small part to its famous college and picture gallery. Gentrification continues apace in East Dulwich in particular. The funky shops of Lordship Lane and Northcross Road are thronging in the afternoon and a plethora of recently opened bars and restaurants ensure the area is just as buzzing at night.

**Map 9
No.1**

Persepolis
28-30 Peckham
High Street
London
SE15 5DT

T: 020 76398007

Open/
10.30am-10pm
Seven days a week

Persepolis

The friendly bunch who run this Peckham High Street bazaar claim to be the largest importers of Persian products in the country. And looking at the dazzling array of Eastern ephemera on display at Persepolis, it's easy to believe that's the case. The majority of the stock here is made up by Iranian and Middle Eastern food (including a fair few fair-trade items), but you'll also find an interesting collection of Persian handicrafts - including some spectacular Shishe pipes - music and books. Probably the most novel thing about the shop though, is that it is - in the words of its owners - 'annotated'. Practically every item has a little yellow label offering a - mostly tongue-in-cheek - explanation of what it is, where it's from, and sometimes how it got there. Not only can these be rather helpful to the uninitiated, they also help to enhance the fun feeling of organised chaos that pervades the store.

Petitou

Bare floorboards, solid furniture and cosy corners are the order of the day in this quality Peckham caff. Existing in an increasingly popular area for bars and brasseries, Petitou faces stiff competition for custom, but fends it off with a winning combination quality food and drink and a homely atmosphere. A number of blackboards dotted around the place announce a regularly rotated menu that features solid salads and robust soups and sarnies – along with more continental offerings like savoury tarts and quiche. If you only try one dish while you're here though, make sure it's a slice of one of the excellent cakes. And wash it down with a rich, strong coffee. Heaven.

Food//

**Map 9
No.2**

Petitou
63 Chourmet Road
London
SE15 4AR

T: 020 7639 2613

Open/
9.am-6pm
Wed-Sat;
10am-6pm, Sun

Food//

Map 9
No.3

East Dulwich Deli
15-17
Lordship Lane
London
SE22 8EW

T: 020 8693 2525

Open/
9am-6pm
Mon-Sat;
10am-4pm, Sun

East Dulwhich Deli

Small, but perfectly formed, the East Dulwich Deli is everything a good delicatessen should be: well-stocked, busy and attended to by knowledgeable and friendly staff. The array of food and drink on offer is everything you'd hope it to be with delicious cold cuts such as Serrano and Parma ham, fine quality English and continental cheeses, olives, roasted vegetables and of course a vast selection of pickles and chutneys to accompany it all. Last year, owners Tracey and Tony, with master baker Manuel Monade, also opened Born & Bread - an excellent artisan bakery - and you'll find their delicious loaves on sale in the deli as well. If we've one complaint it's that the prices sometimes seem a touch expensive – but that really is nit-picking, it's generally hard to find fault with this local favourite.

Review

From a distance you could be mistaken for thinking this splendid bookshop was a café. When the weather's nice there are tables and chairs on the cobbles out front for customers lounge on while they leaf through a prospective purchase and enjoy a free (yes, free!) coffee. The first thing we noticed on entering was that Review also stocks Smoke – a quarterly love letter to London written by and for its inhabitants, and a sure fire indicator of good taste. The books on sale lean towards the high-brow, with plenty of worthy tomes on art, architecture, photography and design – as well as a few classics of literature for ballast. Make your way here on a sunny afternoon to while away a pleasant hour browsing and pick yourself out an enriching read – or just forget the books and concentrate on looking learned...

Entertainment//

Map 9
No.4

Review
28-30 Peckham
High Street
London
SE15 5DT

T: 020 7639 7400

Open/
10am-7pm
Tue-Sun

Hope and
Greenwood
20 North Cross
Road
East Dulwich
London
SE22 9EU

T: 020 8613 1777

www.hopeand
greenwood.co.uk

Open/
10am-6pm
Mon-Sat

Hope and Greenwood

Ok, not everything about Britain in the 1950s was great. We still had rationing, indoor toilets were considered a luxury and closest thing we had to rock 'n' roll rebellion was skiffle. But there was one thing about the post war era that it's worth getting all misty-eyed with nostalgia for - the sweets! In these days of metre-long strings of bubble gum and giant chocolate monstrosities, how refreshing it is to find a good old old-fashioned sweet shop like Hope and Greenwood. The innumerable (well, 175) glass jars that line the walls of this friendly retro emporium are filled with all kinds of colourful, old-time delights from sharp, sherbert-filled flying saucers and powerful cough candy to sickly cola cubes and chewy pontefract cakes. They even do a handsome line in posh, handmade chocolates for grown ups. A dream come true for sweet-toothed shoppers everywhere...

Roullier White

When Lawrence and Philip, the founders of this stylish home store, were struggling to find what they desribe as 'good-quality, everyday items' in the High Street they decided the best course of action was to open their own shop. And so, in November 2005, Roullier White was born. With their impressive array of high-end furniture and accessories for bedroom and basement - and everywhere in between - the chaps aim to bring a touch of the Hamptons to East Dulwich. So whether you're in the market for something indispensable - Egyptian cotton bedding, classic bone china crockery, cast iron cookware - or frivolous - a wine bottle-shaped pepper grinder, toy theatre, retro 1920s horse racing board game - you'll find it here in 'London's only New York-style general store'.

Roullier White
125 Lordship Lane
London
SE22 8HU

T: 020 8693 5150

www.roullierwhite.
co.uk

Open/
10am-6pm
Mon-Sat;
11-4pm, Sun

Map 10

Legend:
- ✱ interesting venue
- ☕ cafe
- 🍺 pub
- Ⓜ market
- Ⓦ wi-fi
- ✗ restaurants
- ⓜ museum
- ⊖ underground
- ⊕ overground

Battersea Telecom
The Greyhound

Latchmere Pub

Battersea Park Road

Battersea Boot, Battersea Technology College

Lavender Rd

North St

Wandsworth Rd

Clapham High St

Falcon Rd

Clapham Junction

Lavender Hill

Cedars Road

Landor Pub

St John's Hill

Battersea Rise

Clapham Common North Side

Clapham High St

Clapham Common

Northcote Road

Webb's Rd

Manor Rd

Clapham Common

Clapham Common South Side

Abbeville Rd

The Ave

Wandsworth Common

Bolingbroke Gr

Nightingale Lane

Clapham South

100m

Getting There/

Buses: 49, 319, 344, 345, 44, 137, 35, 345, 322, 155, 345.
Tube: Clapham Common, Clapham South, Clapham North or Vauxhall. Rail: Clapham Junction; Battersea Park

What's There/

Internet: Battersea.net, 40 St John's Hill; Battersea Telecom, 152 Battersea High Street; Glowlounge, 6 Cavendish Parade; Uniconnect, 20A Clapham Road. Cafes: Boiled Egg & Soldiers, 63 Northcote Road; Crumpet, 66 Northcote Road; The Pavement Café, 21 The Pavement. **Restaurants:** Fish in a Tie, 105 Falcon Road; La Pampa Grill [Argentinian], 60 Battersea Rise; Osteria Antica Bologna, 23 Northcote Road; Gastro Deli Diner, 67 Venn Street; Eco, 162 Clapham High Street. **Pubs:** Latchmere, 503 Battersea Park Road; Greyhound [gastropub with great wine list], 136 Battersea High Street; Nightingale, 95 Nightingale Lane; Bread and Roses, 68 Clapham Manor Street; The Tim Bobbin, 1-3, Lillieshall Rd; The Prince of Wales, 38 Clapham Old Town. **Markets:** Battersea Boot, Battersea Technology College, Battersea Park rd.(Sunday)

Culture/

Festivals: Clapham Festival of Music and the Arts (June-July) Places of Interest: Battersea Power Station; Clapham Picture House, 76 Venn Street. Parks: Battersea Park; Clapham Common. **Museums/Galleries:** Pump House Gallery, Battersea Park; Peace Pagoda, Battersea Park; National Museum of Type, 100 Hackford Road

Battersea, Clapham

Nicknamed 'nappy valley' thanks to the profusion of young families in the area Northcote Road represents the epicentre of this fertile community, while Falcon Road and its environs offer a stark contrast with their imposing estates and trendy hangouts. Clapham, no longer 'up the junction' has become the epitome of upwardly-mobile living. Ignore the High Street – packed with ubiquitous chain stores and bars – and head instead for more interesting side streets such as Abbeville Road, or the Pavement. Take Landor Road to Brixton and explore a variety of cool pubs, cafes and smaller shops.

Doves
71 Northcote Road
London
SW11 6PJ

T: 020 7223 5191

Open/
8am-4pm, Mon
8am-5.30pm
Tue-Sun

Doves

A Dove & Son has been trading as a butcher since the end of the nineteeth century, and crossing the threshold of this proud old institution feels like taking a step back in time. Everything about the place, from the well-scrubbed white tiles to the enthusiatic service, screams of old-fashioned retail values. And no surprise, given that over 100 years of experience goes into all the fabulous free range and organic meat sold here. Current encumbant Bob is always handy with a word of advice on which meat to serve and what cuts to choose - or even just to shoot the breeze about the business in general. Meanwhile, butcher's wife Linda reportedly makes the tasty meat pies herself. If you want a real treat, try the sausages, we've never tasted better.

Verde

Ok, so you're senjoying an indulgent a shopping spree on chi-chi Northcote Road. You've bought your new shoes from Opus, your Creuset from La Cuisiniere, and your flowers from La Maison des Roses - where are you going to go for your luxurious, handmade cosmetics? Why, to Verde, of course! Managing Director Ruby Cook and three former City co-workers set up the company in 1988 as a means of selling products that Ruby had been concoting in her kitchen. The Northcote Road shop opened in 1990 - and the good burghers of Battersea have been thanking them ever since. Favourites such Italian Lemon Hand Cream, Sweet Orange and Geranium Bath Cream and Chamomile Baby Body Cream sound good enough to eat - and, with the mainly organic ingredients used to make them, they might just be. There's another branch at 15 Flash Walk, Hampstead. Go on, spoil yourself.

Health//

Map 10
No.2

Verde
75 Northcote Road
London
SW11 6PJ

T: 020 7223 2095

www.verde.co.uk

Open/
9.30am-6pm
Mon-Sat;
11am-6pm, Sun

La Maison des
Roses
48 Webb's Road
London
SW11 6PJ
T: 020 7228 5700

www.
maisondesroses.
co.uk

Open/
10am-6pm
Mon-Sat

La Maison des Roses

The name says it all, really. This heavily, heavily-scented florist doesn't just specialise in roses - it ONLY sells roses. Roses of every conceivable colour, size and shape in various states - fresh, freeze-dried and preserved (and you thought they only came small, red, and on Valentine's Day). In fact, 'florist' really doesn't do the comfy, friendly boutique justice. La Maison des Roses is more like a temple to the most romantic and beautiful of blooms, and their custom packaging - handmade beaded bags in pretty pastel colours - make each bouquet more like a work of art than a bunch of flowers. Add to this nationwide delivery and bespoke services such as room decoration and you have everything a wannabe Casanova could desire. Their only concession to non-floral products is a range of candles, soaps and room sprays scented with... well, you can probably guess.

Opus Shoes

Open a year and catering principally for the hordes of yummy mummies that populate the more stylish stretch of Battersea's Northcote Road, Opus offers an impressive collection of designer shoes, bags and jewellery. The footwear - encompassing everything from funky trainers by Onitsika Tiger and Puma, Spanish and Italian-designed heels and sandals, ballet pumps and a few indispensable designers like Lulu Guinness - attracts a young, fashion-conscious crowd that seem very much at home in Opus's attractive, shabby-chic showroom. The service, thanks to manager Bernie's easy-going demeanour, is attentive without ever feeling overbearing - so it's a great place to go and browse even if you've not got anything specific in mind.

Fashion//

Map 10 No.4

Opus Shoes
57 Northcote Road
London
SW11 1NP

T:020 7978 4240

www.opusshoes.
co.uk

Open/
10am-5pm
Mon-Tues;
10am-7pm
Wed-Thur;
10am-6pm, Sat
Noon-4pm, Sun

La Cuisiniere
81-83 Northcote
Road
London
SW11 6PJ

T: 020 7223 4409

Open/
9.30am-4pm
Mon-Sat

La Cuisinere

Rapidly approaching its twentieth year of trading, La Cuisiniere is the elder statesman of Northcote Road's numerous lifestyle stores. It specialises in high-quality kitchen equipment that's practical enough to justify the price and stylish enough to impress the neighbours. Whether you're looking for professional-quality knives by the likes of Sabatier and Wurstof; pots and pans from old-fashioned, cast-iron Le Creuset numbers to modern stainless steel by Cuisinox; or your pick of a vast array of kitchen utensils and catering accessories, this sizeable showroom has it all. You can even bring a touch of catering quality to your outdoor dining with a broad range of picnic hampers and cool bags. There's a smaller branch housing the overspill from the main outlet down at 91 Northcote Road.

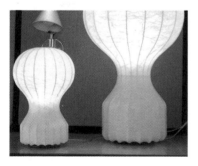

Geoffrey Harris

Watching a re-run of The Italian Job on TV recently we were struck by the spectacular Pier Giacomo Arco lamp that Michael Caine and his fellow felons use to decorate their meeting room. Making it our mission to find one just like it, our search led us to Geoffrey Harris - a shining beacon of a lighting shop on Battersea Park Road. Geoffrey has been selling lighting since he secured his first job with Habitat as a green 17 year old back in 1969. He opened his own showroom in 1999 - and a veritable treasure trove of lamps, shades and accessories it is. Not only did we covet our beloved Arco, we also played with the poseable desk lamps (the classic Anglepoise is a favourite), perused classic Scandinavian shades by Le Klint, and drooled over an impressive range of 20th-century antiques (from the likes of Poole and Whitefriars). Even the basics are catered for with a good stock of bulbs, ceiling roses and flex.

Home//
**Map 10
No.6**

Geoffrey Harris
537 Battersea Park
Road
London
SW11 3BL

www.
geoffreyharris.
co.uk

Open/
10am-6pm
Mon-Sat

Places and Spaces
30 Old Town
London
SW4 0LB

T: 020 7498 0998

www.
placesandspaces.
com

Open/
10.30-6pm
Tues-Sat;
Noon-4pm, Sun
Closed Mon

Places and Spaces

A haven for ultra-modern, uber-stylish furniture and accessories in Clapham's quaint Old Town, Places and Spaces has everything even the most demanding design fascist could wish for. The collection concentrates on the finest contemporary design but is judiciously seasoned with a welcome selection of 20th century classics such as the 1960s Shell chair by Hans Wegner and the peerless 1930s Anglepoise lamp. Among the more eyecatching pieces available were the handgun-shaped bedside lamp designed by Phillipe Starck for Flos and the extravagantly patterned HM17 sofa by null, but our favourite was a rather novel slot-together wooden moose head by Vlaemsch — very witty. Also keep an eye out for the company's own furniture brand Flo, whose doily rug is a delight.

M Moen & Sons

Though a relative youngster at just 35 years old, Moen's is a genuine rival to Battersea's famous Doves in every other respect. Its spacious premises – restored a few years back to its original Victorian grandeur with the aid of a National Lottery grant – houses four counters each packed with the finest in free range and organic meat, own-made sausages, cold cuts and deli items from 60 of the best small producers in the country. And that's not all, to the right as you enter the shop is a wall lined with gourmet pickles, chutneys, mustards and dressings, and in season a daily delivery brings wild mushrooms and a fine selection of fresh fruit and veg. Manager Garry Moen (the son of founder Maurice) and his helpful staff are on hand with expert advice on your choice of joint, but if you want our opinion, you could do worse than to head straight for the excellent game selection.

Food//

Map 10
No.8

M Moen & Sons
24 The Pavement
London
SW4 0JA

T: 020-7622 1624

www.moen.co.uk

Open/
8.30am-6.30pm
Mon-Fri,
8.30am-5pm, Sat

Map 10
No.9

Siecle
789 Wandsworth
Road
London
SW8 3JQ

T: 020 7978 2345

Open/
9.30am-5.30pm
Mon-Sat

Siecle

Born out of a desire to launch an independent paint company that wasn't shackled to the stuffy old chintz and chocolate shades of the likes of Laura Ashley, Siecle is a one-stop decorating shop for forward thinking DIY devotees across the capital. Taking his inspiration from contemporary continental producers – Dutch firms in particular – founder Simon March came up this 'modernist interior paint company' in 2003. The paints, which are all made to his own recipes in the Siecle factory in Northern Holland, bear out his intention to be bright and modern with light, cheerful colours the order of the day. The company also produces its own wallpaper in similarly striking hues. The Clapham branch is exclusively a showroom for the products, but in Waterloo you'll find a Siecle coffee shop where you can browse the collection over a cuppa.

Josephine Ryan

Tucked away on Abbeville Road, a few doors down from flamboyant fashion store Fifi Wilson, is this equally fanciful antiques and interiors outlet. Specialising in 19th-century French furniture, owner Josephine Ryan offers the perfect collection for punters who prefer their homes delicately decorated - and a more classic alternative to fellow Clapham interiors emporium Siecle. So if you picture yourself reclining foppishly on an elegant chaise longue, posing alluringly in the flickering light of an antique chandelier – or just need to locate a fancy little accessory to brighten up your boudoir, pay a visit to Josephine. The welcoming manager is usually around to offer advice and enthusiasm in person. Bring a bit of belle époque grandeur to your gaff.

Home//
**Map 10
No.10**

Josephine Ryan
63 Abbeville Road
London
SW4 9JW

T: 020 8675 3900

www.josephineryan
antiques.co.uk

Open/
10am-6pm
Mon-Sat;
Noon-5pm, Sun

Fifi Wilson

Fifi Wilson
51 Abbeville Road
London
SW4 9JX

T: 020 8675 7775

Open/
10am-6pm
Mon-Sat;
Noon-5pm, Sun

Fi Lovett's adorable Clapham boutique is instantly identifiable by its jolly, candy-striped awning. Inside its a riot of fun, colourful clothes and accessories for style-conscious women and kids (don't worry, it's mainly women). The majority of her clothing collection has a designer shabby-chic feel with lots of floaty floral fare from the likes of Antik Batik, Eucalyptus and Ann-Louise Roswald. The accessories, meanwhile, largely follow suit with Johnny Loves Rosie jewellery, dotty bags by Lulu Guinness and the ubiquitous retro styling of Cath Kidston. Children are well catered for with clothes by Noa Noa and Room Seven and the most key-oot knitted toys by Anne Petit Claire. Strangely though, with all this top-notch gear on display, our favourite items come from the not inconsiderable interiors selection. Among the fabrics and wallpaper you'll find a full range of vintage-style Roberts radios. Indispensable.

The Old Post Office Bakery

Back in the 1980s, German Karl Heinz was so appalled by the quality of the bread baked in the UK that he decided to open his own small organic bakery. Luckily his decision coincided with the first rumblings of a craze for wholefoods and the business quickly took off. It was from these surprisingly pragmatic beginnings that the Old Post Office grew to become one of the most successful organic bakeries in the country. Remaining true to Karl's principles, the shop still bakes only 100% percent organic bread – offering a head-spinning range of loaves – and although the stock has expanded to include a few tasty treats that are not wholly organic, all the cakes, sarnies, pizzas and pastries they sell are made from natural ingredients, without artificial preservatives. No surprise, then, that the bakery is so popular with local office workers at lunchtimes – not to mention several of the biggest organic delivery services in the south east.

The Old Post Office Bakery
76 Landor Road
London
SW9 9PH

T: 020 7326 4408

Open/
9am-6pm
Mon-Sat

The Landor
70 Landor Road
London
SW9 9PH

T: 020 7274 4386

Open/
Noon-11.30pm
Mon-Thur;
Noon-Midnight
Fri-Sat;
Noon-10.30pm
Sun

The Landor

One of the finest pubs in South London and home of the excellent Landor Theatre. If you're feeling a bit pooped after busy afternoon sampling the shopping delights of the Clapham area you could do worse than to treat yourself to a well-deserved pint in this cosily chaotic establishment. Inside you'll find an agreeably haphazard array of furniture and décor (including, we think we're right in saying, an upturned skull hanging from the ceiling!?), and an equally mixed bag of punters – from young, monied trendies to grizzled old locals and most things in between. There are no less than three pool tables to distract you while you slurp your beer, and an appetizing menu packed with comfort food and pub favourites such as burgers, bangers and mash and a cracking Sunday roast. You'll find the theatre upstairs. It's small and intimate and regularly stages productions of a quality to rival the West End. Unmissable.

Mish Mash

Formerly located on the bustling Battersea Park Road, at the time of going to press Mish Mash was in the process of relocating to swanky new premises in Battersea Square It's a location that will well suit the impressive range homeware of this high-end enterprise. Founder Alyson aims to offer a comprehensive service to the houseproud and design-conscious so, as well as the stylish, globally-sourced collection of furniture, lighting, fabrics and accessories you'll find in the showroom, she also offers an interior design service, and even has a team of builders to take on larger tasks. Basically, whether you aim to give your home a top-to-bottom makeover, or if you're just looking for a modest housewarming present – Mish Mash can help. To give you an idea of the quality to expect, let's drop a few names: Pandina lighting, Pilgrim jewellery, Bulgari perfumes and slight seconds of Andrew Martin fabrics and furniture at discounts of 50% or more

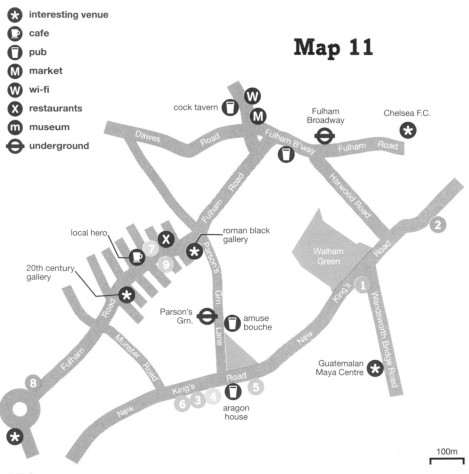

Map 11

Legend:
- ✳ interesting venue
- ☕ cafe
- 🍺 pub
- Ⓜ market
- Ⓦ wi-fi
- ✕ restaurants
- ⓜ museum
- 🚇 underground

cock tavern

Fulham Broadway

Chelsea F.C.

Dawes Road

Fulham B'way

Fulham Road

Harwood Road

local hero

roman black gallery

20th century gallery

Walham Green

Parson's Grn.

Parson's Grn.

amuse bouche

King's Road

Wandsworth Bridge Road

Munster Road

Fulham Road

New King's Road

Guatemalan Maya Centre

aragon house

100m

Getting There/

Buses: 11, 14, 22, 414, 424
Nearest Tube: Parsons Green, Fulham Broadway, Putney Green

What's There/

Internet/wireless: Cock Tavern, 360 North End Road. Cafes: Local Hero (Café) 640 Fulham Road, Pottery Café 735 Fulham Road. Pubs/bars: Aragon House, 247 Kings Road www.aragonhouse.net. Amuse Bouche 51 Parsons Green Lane. Elk Bar 587 Fulham Road. **Restaurants:** Wizzy 616 Fulham Road (Korean) Food: Randalls (Butcher) 113 Wandsworth Bridge Road, London, SW6 2TE. Emporio store 7 New Kings Road. Books:Nomad Books 781 Fulham Road. Markets: North End Road Market Mon-Sat

Culture/

Place of interest/local attraction: Museum of Fulham Palace, Bishop's Avenue, SW6 6EA 020 7736 3233. Chelsea Football Stadium. The Guatemalan Maya Centre 94 Wandsworth Bridge Road SW6 2TF **Museums/ Galleries:** Roman Black Gallery, 600 Fulham Road SW6 5PA. 20th Century Gallery, 821 Fulham Road SW6 5HG. Parks: Walham Green, Parsons Green, South Park, Hurlingham Park, Eel Brook Common.

Fulham, Parsons Green

Fulham's leafy, inviting village ambience is lined with Conker trees and red brick Edwardian and Victorian houses. Populated with dog walkers, the family strollers and maybe the odd celebrity you will stumble across eclectic shops, restaurants and cosy gastro pubs. Meander through our shop listing starting with the infamous Randall's butcher and ending up Catherine of Aragon's old haunt Aragon House. Be independent.

Bullet Motor
Cycles
51 New Kings Rd
London SW6 4SE

T: 020 7736 3811

www.
bulletmotorcycles.
com

Open/
10am-7pm
Mon-Sat;
12pm-4pm, Sun

Bullet Motor Cycles

Exclusive limited edition MV
Augusta's and off-road Yamaha's line
the pavement of this two-floored
motorbike emporium. The BMC
team, James, Roy and Vinnie have
created a very friendly, informative
environment in their garage styled
shop. They stock whatever any
avid motorcyclists desires from
oil, specialist parts, Cromwell
accessories, Triumph motorbike's to
Jeans made from Kevlar (a protective
fabric) and the latest Japanese fad,
the Hit-Air biking airbag jacket. The
scooter skirt by Tucano Urbano is
very popular with their large female
client base as is the special colour
coding service they provide, so your
Vespa scooter or CAT leather helmet
can match your handbag. The boys
are at hand to educate and support
their customers and have created
Moto Concierge, a service that can
arrange anything, from bespoke
items to a breakdown emergency
service. Having sponsored the 'Long
Way Round', Charley Boorman and
Ewan McGregor's famous bike ride,
you know you are in safe hands.

Megan's Deli

This exceptional deli is laid over two floors in a higgledy piggledy fashion. Originally an Antique shop, owner Megan decided to save the hell of the sandwich lunch hour and create a little piece of her New Zealand homeland. With a huge choice of freshly cooked delectable food, you are encouraged to mix up the buffet style menu. Expect salads of green beans, almonds, bacon and shallots; sweet potato and coconut soup, beef and horseradish tart or the signature dish Chicken Marbella, which is marinated chicken in white wine and prunes. You can relax in the picturesque enclosed garden with a slice of the scrumptious wheat free chocolate brownie or take home freshly baked gluten free bread and a pot of nectarine and passion fruit jam for tea. Everyone is catered for at Megan's as they are vegetarian friendly and allergy conscious. They extend their services and can cater for weddings, birthdays and corporate events or hire out the garden for anything from hen nights to gallery opening after parties.

Food//

Map 11
No.2

Megan's Deli
571 Kings Road
London SW6

T: 020 7371 7837

Open/
8am-6pm
Mon-Sat;
10am-4pm, Sun

Marc Wallace

Marc Wallace
261 New Kings Rd
Fulham
London
SW6 4RB

T: 020 7736 6795
Appointments:
020 7731 4575

www.marcwallace.
com

Open/
10am-6pm
Tue-Sat;
12pm-5pm, Sun;
Thursday
late night by
appointment only

Marc Wallace set up his eponymous menswear label and showroom 7 years ago. The warmly decorated interior has rails of romantically coloured suits, slim cut trousers in a steely palette, floral waistcoats and bright fuscia shirts hanging next to Old-fashioned cabinets displaying leather wallets, cuff links, socks, classically hand-crafted shoes and silk ties. Offering ready to wear, bespoke and hire pieces, it is his colourful signature floral design that sets him apart from other designers. It appears on the lining of jackets, inside shirt collars, on the reverse of a tie, the inner sole of shoes and all over the very popular jersey boxers, which by the way make for a great pressie.

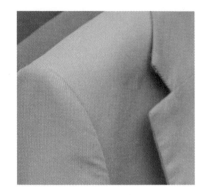

Harmer

Leigh Harmer had a desire to get back to his creative roots providing an outlet for well-designed sofas, lighting and accessory items, so back in 2002 he moved from his Shoreditch shopfront to Parsons Green. His passion for modern design is evident in the innovative timeless products displayed by up and coming designers. Sophistication oozes from the vibrant showroom as you meander past the popular Esprit sofa system, stylish pieces by Irish talent Garvan de Bruir and chance upon the sculptural Shakti floor light by Marzio Rusconi. With a growing team of Interior Designer's Harmer offers a number of services from Product Loan, Interior Consultations, Bespoke & Made to Measure Design to the recently launched Harmer @ Home, the live-in, working, Interior Design portfolio for clients to experience a true-to-life feel of contemporary living.

Home//

Map 11 No.4

Harmer
253 New Kings Rd
Parsons Green
London
SW6 4RB

T: 020 7736 5111

www.harmer.
uk.com

Open/
10am-6.30pm
Mon-Thurs;
10am-6pm
Fri-Sat;
12pm- 5pm Sun;
Afterhours
appointment on
T: 020 7736 5111

Pugs & Kisses
183 New Kings Rd
Parsons Green
London
SW6 4SW

T: 020 7731 0098

www.
pugsandkisses.
com

Open/
10am-6pm
Mon-Sat

Pugs & Kisses

What more could your pooch or kitty cat ask for than their very own luxury boutique. American owner Candace has brought a little bit of Stateside glamour to Parsons Green. Filled with an array of accessories and its very own spa, your pup will be in seventh heaven. You can treat your Bichon Frises to a fashionable ribbon lead by American import Bella Bean or your Yorkshire Terrier to hand baked iced cookies. While you choose a bed made out of beautiful patterned fabric for your Persian, downstairs your Daschund can have a full groom in the relaxing spa. A session will cost you anything from £30 to £95 and can include a, manicure, pedicure, shampoo, ear cleaning, brush out, aromatherapy freshening spritz and fluff dry and styling. The only thing left is for a Dog walking service and guess what that's coming soon!

Deuxieme

Fancy second-hand fashion with a glamorous streak and potential money making tip to boot? Well Deuxieme provides just that, take your unwanted wardrobe items along and they will keep your discarded treasures for up to 8 weeks taking 50% on any sold items. Camilla, who trained as an Actress, took over 5 years ago because of her shear passion for fashion. Emphasis is on designer clothing and accessories with the odd vintage piece. Both floors of this emporium are filled from floor to ceiling with something for everyone from rails of cocktail dresses, slim-line skirts, silky tops to skinny jeans, bejewelled capes, stilettos and 70's inspired sunglasses but it is Designer handbags that are the most sort after item, so if you have a penchant for Vintage Chanel or Louis Vuitton, you're in the right place.

Fashion//

Map 11
No.6

Deuxieme
299 New Kings Rd
London SW6

T: 020 7736 3696

Open/
10am-6pm
Mon-Sat;
11am-5pm, Sun

Map 11 No.7

Indian Summer
624c Fulham Rd
Parsons Green
London SW6

T: 020 7731 8234

www.indian
summershop.com

Open/
10am-6.30pm
Mon-Sat;
12pm-5pm, Sun

Indian Summer

Indian Summer is a treasure trove of worldly delights brought to you by travelling friends Ruth and Karin. Opened in 2004, the lifestyle boutique is based on the duo's passions for carefully chosen items they fall in love with from all over the world. With lots of one off pieces like the Sami quilts made by the Sami gypsies of India or the Handerias, from the Atlas Mountains worn as wraps by the Nomads, the shop is full of exceptional items. With their experimental buying style there is an eclectic mix of old Indian furniture, hand painted tins, beauty products, cushion, lamps, candles, Moroccan boots, Gold charm necklaces and toy bears. They recently launched their own fashion line featuring Kaftan's, Cashmere bolero's and the effortlessly stylish Rope Dress. You can even take home a little piece of Indian Summer, in the form of the shops signature scent Ambre de Indien by French company Esteban.

Copes Seafood Co.

Adam Yilmaz has firmly anchored himself as fishmonger extraordinaire in Fulham with his marvelous seafood establishment. Run on the old fashioned Mediterranean ethos of using what ever is caught that day, fresh fish arrives from his small environmentally friendly suppliers after a 6-hour drive from the coast. There is a wide variety on offer of Cornish Cod, John Dory, Squid, Monkfish, Halibut, Lemon Sole, Turbet, Brill, Octopus and Ray Wings. However you must sample from their specialties; Sea Urchins or the Cuttlefish Ink, which is perfect for creating a unique Risotto or Pasta. The in-house Italian Chef makes up fresh crab balls and a selection of fishcakes on a daily basis, as well as gravlax, bouillabaisse and pate. They also give recipe suggestions, will order in requests, can cook the fish for you to collect after a long hard day at work and can even make sashimi for that last minute Sushi party you might be throwing.

Food//

Map 11 No.8

Copes Seafood Co.
778 Fulham Road
London SW6

T: 020 7371 7300

Open/
9.30am-7.30pm
Mon-Fri;
9am-7pm, Sat

Map 11 No.9

Mind, Body & Spirit
755 Fulham Road
London
SW6 5UU

T: 020 7731 2828

www.mindbody
spiritdirect.co.uk

Open/
10am-6pm,
Mon-Sat

Mind, Body & Spirit

Looking for that inner calm, spiritual inspiration or maybe just a gemstone, well look no further, Mel Donovan and his alternatively trained expert team are at the ready to put you in touch with some of the world's most inspirational teachers and artists. Specialising in personal empowerment products, display cabinets and shelves are over flowing with Meditation books, Yoga DVD's, Whale song CD's, Energy and healing kits, oil burners and Chakra jewellery. They are widely known for their amazing selection of crystals that decorate a large area of the shop and the extraordinary array of Buddha's in all shapes, sizes and colours imported from Thailand. They will give advice and source items if you request something they don't have in stock. If you are too overwhelmed by the plethora of products on offer then you can purchase gift vouchers so a loved one can do there own searching for a stress-free life.

di·ver·si·ty

a variety of something such as opinion, colour, or style

Map 12

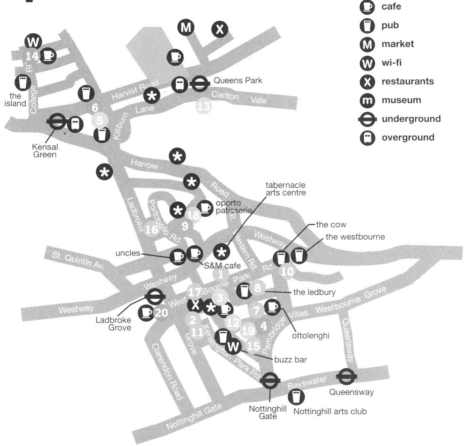

Legend

- ✱ interesting venue
- ☕ cafe
- 🍺 pub
- Ⓜ market
- Ⓦ wi-fi
- ⊗ restaurants
- Ⓜ museum
- ⬤ underground
- 🔲 overground

Map labels

the island

Queens Park

Carlton Vale

Harvist Road

Lane

Killburn

Kensal Green

College Rd.

Harrow Road

Ladbroke Grove

Portobello Rd.

St. Quintin Av.

tabernacle arts centre

oporto patisserie

the cow

the westbourne

Westway

uncles

S&M cafe

the ledbury

Westbourne Park Rd.

Westway

Westway

Ladbroke Grove

ottolenghi

Westbourne Grove

Pembridge Villas

Queensway

West Bourne Park

Kensington Park Rd.

Pembridge

buzz bar

Clarendon Road

Grove

Bayswater

Queensway

Nottinghill Gate

Nottinghill Gate

Nottinghill arts club

Getting There/

Bus: 7,12, 23,27, 28, 31, 70, 94, 328 Kensal Rise 6, 18, 28, 52, 187, 302, 316. Tube: Notting Hill Gate, Ladbroke Grove, Holland Park, Kensal Green, Queens Park. **Trains:** Kensal Rise

What's There/

Internet: Kitchen & Pantry; Gracelands (free Wi-Fi). **Cafes:** Tom's, 226 Westbourne Grove; 202, 202 Westbourne Grove; Ottolenghi, 287 Ledbury Rd; Uncles, 305 Portobello Rd; Oporto Patisserie (Portuguese), 62a Golborne Road; Electric Cinema (brasserie w/crèche), Portobello rd.; **Pubs:** The Cow, 89 Westbourne Park Rd; Notting Hill Arts Club, 21 Notting Hill Gate; Trailer Happiness (cool lounge bar), 177 Portobello Rd; Paradise by Way of Kensal Green, 19 Kilburn Lane; The Island, 123 College Road, NW10; Greyhound, 64-66 Chamberlayne Rd. **Restaurants:** Food @ The Muse, 269 Portobello Rd; Sausage and Mash Café, 268 Portobello Rd; The Ledbury, 127 Ledbury Rd; E&O (asian), 14 Blenheim Crescent; Hugo's, 21-25 Lonsdale Rd NW6. Markets: Portobello Market [Mon-Sat] Queen's Park Farmers' Market, Sundays 10am-2pm,Salusbury Rd

Culture/

Festivals: Notting Hill Carnival, bank holiday weekend in August. Portobello Film Festival July-August. Place of interest/local attraction: Moroccan area/ Golborne rd Tabernacle arts center, Powis square (facing uncertain future) Lucho Brieva House and Showroom 213 Kilburn Lane. The Electric Barge (party barge for hire), 453 Harrow Rd. **Museums/Galleries:** The Dissenters' Gallery, Kensal Green Cemetery; London Print Studio, 425 Harrow Road. **Parks:** Hyde Park, Queens Park

Notting Hill, Kensal Rise

Notting Hill itself has changed a lot over the past decades. 50 years ago it was the heart of the West Indian windrush and this heritage is still a vital part of the area. However, it has also become incredibly gentrified hence the manicured vision in Hugh Grant and Julia Roberts' romcom 'Notting Hill'. Yet the area still retains pockets of Moroccan (Golborne rd) and West Indian culture that give the area some life. It still has some great independent shops too. Kensal Rise with lots of intriguing shops, and The Dissenters' Chapel as an unlikely exhibition space, make NW6 a must to be explored.

Map 12
No.1

The Jackson Twins
5 All Saints Road
London
W11 1HA

T: 02077928336

www.thejacksons.
co.uk

Open/
11am-6pm,
Mon-Fri
11am-6pm, Sun

The Jackson Twins

All Saints Road has changed a lot over the past 15 years. Once the most notorious and violent street in Notting Hill, its gone full circle and became one of the most posh ones brimming with independent boutiques and restaurants. The Jackson Twins opened in 1998 at number 5. It was started by ex-fashion PR Joey Jackson and sister Louise who trained in theatre design. Louise began designing scarves in 1995 and the siblings soon got together to form accessories label The Jackson Twins. This crowded little shop at the front of their head office is a bit like a French atelier. It sells their wares which range from raffia bags with an ethnic feel to slick olive suede knee length boots and vintage style sandals, as well as hats and scarves.

Cocoribbon

Cocoribbon has been open since 2002 and it quickly became one of Notting Hills musts. The shop was opened by two fashion PRs Sophie Oliver and Australian Alison Chow and many of the labels stocked are from down under. They sell everything from bath and body products, perfume, dressing tables and furniture, chiffon panties, and superb evening wear in a myriad of colours. One of the nicest little decorative gifts are their sell out strings of pastel butterflies, made from painted feathers. Famous faces flock in their droves including Jude Law, Sienna Miller, Lily Cole and Jools Oliver. A second branch of this delightful store is on the Chelsea end of Sloane Street.

Fashion//

Map 12
No.2

Cocoribbon
21 Kensington
Park Road
London
W11 2EU

www.cocoribbon.
com

Open/
10am-6pm,
Mon-Sat
12.30-5.30pm, Sun

Ceramica Blue
10 Blenheim
Crescent
London
W11 1NN

T: 02077270288

www.
ceramicablue.
co.uk

Open/
10am-6.30pm,
Mon - Sat
12:00 - 16:00, Sun

Ceramica Blue

Founded in 1987, Ceramica Blue
specialises in handmade and hand
painted ceramics from the cream of
international potteries. The focus is
on pieces that are both functional
and decorative. If you have a kitchen
or dining room, you'll find something
for it here. Items include Japanese
glazed plates, stone table mats
and French bowls. It's not all china
– there's bamboo, stone and glass
pieces too. You could fill your kitchen
with their rustic tableware, mugs,
espresso cups, teapots and tiles.
From vibrant dinner sets in deep
autumnal colours to subtle dishes
with asymmetric rims, this is the
dream gift store for weddings
or foodies. They also happily
ship abroad.

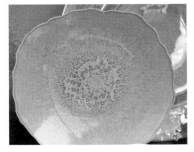

186

Tea Palace

There's nothing old fashioned about the Tea Palace. This gleaming, cleanly designed yet intimate tea shop in the heart of Westbourne Grove's posh area idolizes all things tea related. The cream and white interior is more Vogue than ye olde tea room – though they do a mean scone. There's a restaurant with seasonal food served for breakfast, lunch and, of course, teatime. The main attention is the tea – and they sell every kind possible (even filling their reusable tea caddies and cartons if you're feeling green). The staff will happily help you through the huge selection from Lavender infusions to White tea and there are tea tastings if you want to try some Sultan tea first hand. This decorative palace is also good for gifts with decorative teapots and accessories.

Food//

Map 12 No.4

Tea Palace
175 Westbourne
Grove
London
W11 2SB

T: 020 7727 2600

www.teapalace.com

Open/
10am-7pm
Mon-Sat ,
10am-6.30pm Sun

Niche
70 Chamberlayne
Road
London
NW10 3JJ

T: 020 3181 0081

Open/
10.30am-5.30pm
Tue-Sat

Niche

Polly adores antiques and inspired by visiting her Grandmother's house as a little girl, the passion culminated in opening Niche ten months ago. The shop is full of things that she loves from French and English furniture, Edwardian vintage paintings, lamps, antique jewellery to just about anything that catches her eye, quirky or not. Her signature items are Tala 1930-50's kitchenware that ranges from £5-50 and household items like stunning Enamel 1940's kitchen tables. Vintage sign letters along with angel poised lamps fly out of the door. Polly's background in property refurbishment holds her in good stead to be able to spot the perfect item for your home. I mean who wouldn't want an English Victorian chest in the bedroom or express their decadence through hanging a French chandelier in the dinning room.

Scarlett & Violet

Opened six months ago out of frustration for the perfect flower shop, Victoria Brotherson's has successfully created just that. Taking her 13 years of floristry experience, fine art background and Cumbrian upbringing, customers are in for a treat of textually based flower bouquets and arrangements. From Hydrandgea's to Yellow Lillies, Victoria produces a loose garden feel with a hint of embroidery. She offers anything from gift bunches to weddings displays. Although the highlight of Scarlett and Violet must be the ingenious combination of being able to buy a vintage vase complete with a bunch of flowers. Choose from the eclectic selection of beautiful porcelain on display in the old wooden Victorian cabinets for the perfect Mother's Day treat or romantic gesture.

Flowers//

Map 12
No.6

Scarlett & Violet
76 Chamberlayne
Road
London
NW10 3JJ

T: 020 8969 9446

scarletandviolet@b
tinternet.com

Open/
8.30am-6pm,
Mon-Fri
8.30am-5pm, Sat
11am-3pm Sun
Times can vary
slightly.

Map 12
No.7

Aime
32 Ledbury Road
London
W11 2AB

T: 020 72217070

www.aimelondon.com

Open/
10.30am-7pm
Mon-Sat

Aime

The fabulously French concept shop Aimé is one of London's best secret addresses. Run by French-Cambodian sisters Val and Vanda Heng-Vong, the small two floor shop sells the cream in contemporary French womenswear from labels that are hard to find this side of the channel. There are fluid dresses from Antik Batik and Isabel Marant, tailoring from Les Prairies de Paris and Claudie Pierlot, ballet shoes from Repetto and one of the best selections of APC in London. In addition to the clothes, half the shop is devoted to design, with hand made ceramics and glassware on the beautiful peaceful cream shelves. There are also gifts from CDs to scents and Aime's own range of scented candles. (They also do a killer twice yearly sale where many things are 50% off). Arriving at Aimé is like hopping on the Eurostar without the hassle.

Alice & Astrid

This tiny narrow shop with pastel painted wooden floors resembles the front room of someone's home that's been transformed into a little den of all things pretty. Products include pretty blue pillows, full of hanging butterflies, polka dots, chiffon underwear, the ubiquitous scented candle, and girly gym bags. Many of the pieces are from the store's own label including baby alpaca knits, brushed cotton nightshirts and delicate printed textiles. The shop opened in 2003 and clients include Kristen Scott Thomas, Laura Bailey and even the British Royals. Everything feels pretty and feminine in here – like the décor of a boudoir every girl imagines when young. It makes it perfect for gifts and the staff are delightful.

Fashion//
Map 12
No.8

Alice & Astrid
30 Artesian Road
London
W2 5DD

T: 020 7985 0888

www.
aliceandastrid.com

Open/
Mon-Sat,
11am-6pm

Beverley Knowles
Fine Art
88 Bevington Road
London W10 5TW

T: 020 8969 0800

www.
beverleyknowles.
com

Open/
11am-6pm,
Tue-Sat

Beverley Knowles Fine Art

Sister are doing it for themselves at Beverley Knowles. The gallery on the corner of Golborne Road, was founded in 2002 and has been in this space for two years. The space focuses solely on British female artists garnered from colleges across the country. The clean white space, which isn't too over minimalist, has a feminist mindset and the work itself isn't too in your face. There's also a ceramics stall on nearby Goldborne Road selling pieces by female ceramicists every Friday and Saturday with bargain prices starting at £10. They also hold evening classes for pro and beginners who want to get to grips with drawing or portraitures over a glass of wine.

Pistol Panties

When it comes to swimwear few people have a better pedigree than designer Deborah Fleming. Born in Paris and raised in Miami, her bikinis and cheeky bottoms perfectly fuse the well made decadence of France with the sexy edge of beach life. Her hip flagship store reflects the retro edge in a lot of the swimwear pieces – inspired by Joan Collins in her heyday no less. Expect lots of frills and polka dots with names like Le Pin Up and Femme Fatale. They also sell vintage beachwear and jewellery sourced by Rellik. Lying in the sun never looked so sexy.

Fashion//
**Map 12
No.10**

Pistol Panties
75 Westbourne
Park Road
London
W2 5QH

T: 020 7229 5286

www.pistolpanties.
com

Open/
Noon-6pm,
Tue-Sat, Sun
1pm-5pm

London
Beach Store
23 Kensington
Park Road
London
W11 2EU

T: 020 7243 2772

www.londonbeach
store.co.uk

Open/
10am-6.30pm,
Mon, Wed, Fri
10am-5.30pm, Tue
10am-7.30pm, Thu
9.30am-6.30pm,
Sat

London Beach Store

If you surf, you've already been to
the London Beach Store. For many
years this was the only place that
was dedicated to that decidedly non-
London sport. The shop (part owned
by fashion photographer David Sims)
is brimming with experts who will
happily help beginners and pros
alike purchase long boards, short
boards, beach wear and everything
else you'd need for extreme sports.
They also have a skateboard section
if you want to get urban, and a good
selection of surf and skate clothing
labels that are especially good for
boys. This popular store manages to
perfectly crossover between technical
advice and a place where laid back
people go to buy a pair of flip flops.

Gong

If you like oriental interiors visit Gong. This dark store with largely Chinese furniture and decorative items is one of Portobello Road's best modern interior shops. Opened seven years ago, this is a treasure trove for people looking for that cosy but cool living or bedroom. There are musky scented candles, lots of black lacquer boxes and shelves, Chinese playing card sets, dark leather seats, blue ceramic bowls and plates, picture frames, and sculptural Buddhas to watch over it all. The shop also specialised in silk lamps in warm colours, made to measure wood furniture and has an interior design service if you just want to hand everything over to them to create for you.

Home//

**Map 12
No.12**

Gong
142 Portobello
Road
London
W11 2DZ

T: 02075654162

www.gong.co.uk

Open/
10am-6pm
Mon-Sun

Davda
342 Kilburn Lane
Queens Park
London
W9 3EF

t: 020 8969 3239

www.
brickettdavda.com

Open/
10am-6pm
Mon-Fri;
11am-6pm Sat

Davda

There is the air of elegance to Davda set up by ceramicists' husband and wife team, Mair and Jo. With their fine art background and 12 years of experience, the shop opened 3 years ago. The minimally decorated interior is cluttered with beautifully coloured ceramics that are crafted in the metal and ceramic workshop out back. Ranging from ceramic tableware to custom made lighting, each piece combines the idea of colour and tactility and warmth from Mair's Morrocan upbringing and Jo's love of European design. Their popular cups and ceramic table range from £10-£60 and the very sculptural folded lighting are anything from £40 upwards. Uniquely elegant each product combines hard edge aesthetics with a softer organic feel. With their every changing collection, keep an eye out for handpainted children's plates, the bottle chandelier and customised blankets. They even work to individual commission; one can but imagine the joy that they could create.

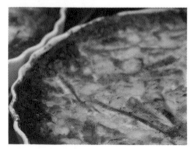

Gracelands

Tiane and James were local parents who didn't have anywhere to go with their children, so they set up Gracelands café a year and half ago. Successfully creating a very homely setting with large wooden tables, where you can wile away the time, checking your emails on the free Wi-Fi, with or without the kids (there is a play area to entertain them). The scrumptious menu comprises a selection of salads, quiche's, goat's cheese terrine, mixed mezze platter, and in winter, stews and curries are rustled up. They even have their own local mother who bakes the cakes; chocolate, carrot and interestingly courgette. On Saturday's, you can get a massage while waiting for your Eggs Benedict or full English to arrive. The walls are adorned with local artists painting that are for sale along with fabric bags, toys, pretty brocade dresses and knickknacks from the 70's. In the autumn they will be opening in the evenings with a licensed and simple restaurant and the renowned Summer Fayre will be returning in 2007.

Food//

Map 12 No.14

Gracelands
118 College Road
London
NW10 5HD

T: 020 8964 9161

www.
gracelandscafe.
com

Open/
9am-5pm, Mon-Fri;
9am-4pm Sat;
9.30am-3pm Sun.

Jessie Western
82b Portobello Rd
London
W11 2QD

T: 020 7229 2544

www.jessie
western.com

Open/
Daily 10am-6pm

Jessie Western

You can go cow-boy (or cow-girl) crazy at Jessie Western. This store is devoted to all things Western. There's an amazing range of silver and turquoise jewellery, often antique pieces sourced for Navajo and Zuni Indians, and some hefty belts with stunning semi-precious stones. This is also the only store in Europe to stock real bespoke Texan boots – and expect some amazing bright patterns and leathers ranging from frog to crocodile! Each boot is hand cut for your feet and takes 10 weeks to make. If that's not enough you could get a bit 'Brokeback Mountain' in some Colorado cowboy hats, embroidered shirts or buy native American artworks bought straight from reservations.

Olivia Morris

How do you combine glamour with humour? Classic style with innovation? Shoe designer Olivia Morris knows. This black super sexy shop at the far end of Portobello is a decadent den devoted to footwear. Her brilliant pieces have ranged from shoes you have to colour in with paint sets to polka dotted wedges that would leave Dita von Teese panting. The prices are pretty steep (£200 plus) but the leather and canvas pieces are impeccably made. Pieces range from red or leopard print laced shoe boots, the perfect court shoe with a chain ankle strap and deep red mary janes.

Fashion//
Map 12
No.16

Olivia Morris
355 Portobello Rd
London W10 5SA

T: 020 8962 0353

www.oliviamorris
shoes.com

Open/
Wed-Sat
11-6pm,
or by appointment

Theirnibs
214 Kensington
Park Road
London
W11 1NR

T: 020 7221 4263

www.theirnibs.
co.uk

Open/
9.30-6pm,
Mon-Fri,
10am-6pm,Sat
12-5pm, Sun

Theirnibs

These days kid's fashion could beat adults in the style stakes. Baby boutique Theirnibs transformed an old chemist into a bright area shop that sells designer clothes for kids 0 to 10 with an emphasis on classic style and heavy prints with an original edge. Not surprisingly celebs from Kate Moss to Jools Oliver love to dress their kids in these wearable prairie dresses and comfy knits. The press trip over themselves to praise the shop which also sells vintage children's clothes as well as Theirnibs own label. In addition to clothes they have cowboy print blankets to keep babies cosy and have lots of space for you to wheel in your pushchair and leave the children in the spacious play area while you focus on clothes.

53AM

Hairdressers Angela Tomlin and Justin Man set up 53AM almost three years ago. The pair had lived, worked and socialised in West London for over a decade and setting up their own shop there was a natural progression. This reasonable hairdresser's has a very laid back vibe with extra friendly staff. The shop itself retains its old wooden front, but the minimalist long interior is peppered only with mirrors and subtle graffiti on the walls. Expect lots of local music and media mavens popping in from their nearby homes. Services are sweet and simple with cuts costing £33 for ladies and £29 for men, a huge amount of colouring from washes to highlights if you want to spice things up.

Health//
Map 12
No.18

53AM
53 Golborne Road
London
W10 5NR

T: 020 8969 2905

Open/
Tue, Sat 9.30-6pm,
Wed-Fri 9.30-7pm

Health//
Map 12
No.19

Beauty Works West
8-9 Lambton Place
Notting Hill
London
W11 2SH

T: 020 7221 7872

www.beautyworks
west.com

Open/
10am-8pm,
Mon-Fri
10am-6pm,
Sat-Sun

Beauty Works West

This creamy calm beauty hotspot
is guaranteed to leave you
relaxed, buffed and beautiful.
BeautyWorksWest is a hidden in
a quiet nook of Notting Hill and
focused on the fusion of science
and beauty. There are traditional
treatments from osteopathy to body
scrubs but this peaceful place also
has specials like O2 treatments and
photo-rejeuvenation, an anti-sun
damage treatment. Their in-house
specialist Dr Daniel Sister who's
treated half of Hollywood will also
see patients about everything from
blue veins to weight loss to a little
liposuction. There's also a great range
of Men Only treatments from manly
manicures to yeti hair removal.

Tea's Me

The only teasing going on here is undoubtedly of the taste variety. This trendy café was once one of the classic Portuguese cafes that fill the area. Its fresh makeover of this sweet old fashion space only compliments the classic vibe of the original spot that stood here. The space is small but cosy with great original Portuguese dishes like salt cod bacalhau alongside classic British fry-ups at bargain prices. The tasty cakes are the main attraction to this friendly spot – be sure to try the obligatory custard tarts for a touch of the Algarve.

Food//
Map 12
No.20

Tea's Me
129a Ladbroke
Grove
London
W11 1PN

T:020 7792 5577

Open/
8am-7pm
Mon-Sat

Index

Acknowlegements

www.independentlondon.com

First published in 2006 by Monstermedia

All rights reserved Effie Fotaki & Moritz Steiger ©2006

Photography by Effie Fotaki & Moritz Steiger ©2006
www.effiefotaki.com, www.steiger.co.uk

Design by HarrimanSteel. www.harrimansteel.co.uk

Printed in Italy by EuroGrafica S.p.A

Contributing Writers: Dean Irvine, Sarah Jacobs,
Richard Lines, Freire Barnes, Francesca Gavin

Very grateful to Mr John Scott for his invaluable support as well as
congratulating him on his plans for an independent shop in Notting Hill,
a small but significant gesture in the face of 'cloneisation' on an epic scale in
the area and also David McHugh of Notting Hill Arts Club for all his advice
and support. David and Zoe at the PR Office...of course a big thanks to anyone
else that has supported us throughout this project; our families; Pantelis,
Achilleas, Peri Fotaki, Rene, Esther and the alpacas in Italy and of course Ursula
Steiger for listening...And finally, thank you. If we have missed out anyone,
please accept our apologies

Moritz & Effie